STUDIES IN CHRISTIAN LIVING

HENRY H. MEYER, Editor
WADE CRAWFORD BARCLAY, Associate Editor

ALCOHOL
AND THE NEW AGE

An Elective Course for Young People

By
DEETS PICKETT

Approved by the Committee on Curriculum
of the Board of Education of the
Methodist Episcopal Church

THE METHODIST BOOK CONCERN
NEW YORK   CINCINNATI

CONTENTS

CHAPTER		PAGE
	EDITOR'S INTRODUCTION	5
I.	THE ADVENTURE OF YOUTH	7
II.	ALCOHOL THE MOCKER	17
III.	HOW ALCOHOL SUBDUED THE RACE	27
IV.	QUESTIONS THAT MAY ARISE THIS VERY DAY	37
V.	THE PRICE OF CIVILIZATION	47
VI.	NEW PROBLEMS IN A NEW WORLD	59
VII.	THE ECONOMIC BENEFITS OF PROHIBITION	69
VIII.	DRINK IN POLITICS	77
IX.	THE BIRTH OF A NEW POLICY	87
X.	IN THE FOOTSTEPS OF STATESMEN	97
XI.	THE QUESTION OF BEER AND WINE	107
XII.	THE CHRISTIAN AND THE LAW	117
XIII.	HOW TO HELP	127
	BIBLIOGRAPHY	135

EDITORS' INTRODUCTION

CONSTITUTIONAL prohibition has brought a new day to the nation. It has induced profound social changes. Licensed saloons, on the main streets of cities, towns, and villages, thronged at all hours of the day and late into the night with men and boys, with the consumption of immense quantities of alcoholic liquors, and the thousand and one accompanying social ills, have gone—gone, we believe, forever. The social and economic benefits of prohibition are many and indisputable. It is easy for the foes of prohibition to weave tissues of lies concerning an increase of drinking among the young, but these are so palpably false upon their face that they deceive few. The facts are so numerous, so easily discoverable, and so convincing that fair-minded people are not likely to be led astray by the distorted and misleading propaganda with which many of the newspapers of the nation have been filled. Enforcement of prohibition has been imperfect and lax, particularly in the large cities, just as the enforcement of many other laws is partial. As a result it has been possible for those intent upon procuring liquor in violation of the law to get it. Because of this and various other new factors new conditions have arisen.

Constitutional prohibition was the result of a long process of education. Since its enactment a new generation has come upon the stage of action. The children of this new generation are now in our schools and church schools. To-morrow they will be voters, determining the future of prohibition as of all other social legislation.

The textbook *Alcohol and the New Age* has been written in view of these conditions. It is the first of a number of courses to be prepared for use in our church schools. It has been written by a specialist whose long study of the subject qualifies him in a special way to write authoritatively. It is to be hoped that the textbook will have the extensive use in study groups of young people that its importance warrants.   THE EDITORS.

But we made our prayer unto our God, and set a watch against them day and night, because of them.

.   .   .   .

And I looked, and rose up, and said unto the nobles, and to the rulers, and to the rest of the people, Be not ye afraid of them: remember the Lord, who is great and terrible, and fight for your brethren, your sons, and your daughters, your wives, and your houses.   (Neh. 4. 9, 14.)

Remember also thy Creator in the days of thy youth, before the evil days come, and the years draw nigh, when thou shalt say, I have no pleasure in them.   (Eccl. 12. 1.)

I have written unto you, young men, because ye are strong. (1 John 2. 14b.)

CHAPTER I

THE ADVENTURE OF YOUTH

In no other time and in no other country have the destinies of the people and the leadership of the race been so completely committed to youth as they are in America at the present time. America is to-day what its young people make it. Far more important is the fact that the America of to-morrow will be what its young people of to-day decide now that it shall be. It is more nearly correct to say that youth *is* the future than to say that it is the master of the future. The nation's future, as represented by the youth of to-day, is the recognized reward that lies gleaming before the contending social groups of the country. Let adults and young people join in considering the present American emergency from the standpoint of youth.

Youth and the Present Emergency

The power of youth.—Wealth means power, and the world never before saw such abounding wealth as we have in America to-day. This wealth is represented by an immense increase in the number and character of material comforts, labor-saving devices, and by machinery of limitless possibilities. When our grandparents were young, their range of activity was limited by the possibilities of the family horse. They knew few people who lived more than five miles distant. To-day young people can step into a sixty-horsepower automobile, have dinner a hundred miles away, and sleep at home. The radio has put them into constant touch with a nation-wide program of entertainment. All this is stimulating in the extreme. But if temptations are multiplied by modern complexities of life, by the fact that so many young people have extended the horizon of their activities and incalculably increased their power, is it not also true that the young people of to-day, because of the increase of machinery and power, are facing a vastly greater responsibility and more numerous opportunities for service to the world? Shall young people make these new instruments "serve the present age" under their direction or shall they be dazed by the perplexities of modern life and destroyed by a new power they cannot use?

The leisure of youth.—Another feature of the situation is the greater leisure of youth to-day. Parents who have been relieved from the grinding oppression of poverty have an intense desire to shield their children from the necessity of hard labor and restricted opportunities for play. The result is that frequently the new idea is over-done; young people are not afforded the opportunity to learn what responsibility means or to know the joy of labor that brings fruit in accomplishment. The young person of a generation ago trudged many miles to school, studied from an unattractive textbook, and labored during the hours that are now devoted to play. In these days parents ask only reasonable devotion to the studies that our modern schools have already lightened by every possible device of recreational interest. The hours after school are usually free. Holidays are free. The long summer months demand only the most casual labor from the average young person. There is greater leisure, and leisure also means power. It is hardly a matter of wonder that such young people as are without ideals or ambition use this leisure in a way that brings discredit upon all young people. What do your leisure moments mean to you, to your home, to your church, to your country, to your God? Does increased leisure make you better or worse?

Seeing flaws.—Two men were walking down the streets of one of our cities when one of them, a bricklayer, turned to his companion and, pointing to a wall, said, "That wall is crooked."

"I can't see it," said his friend.

"Put one eye on the lower right-hand corner," instructed the bricklayer, "and the other eye on the upper left-hand corner."

His friend did so and immediately confirmed the statement that the wall was crooked.

The next day they walked down the street together again. The man who the first day had been unable to see the flaw in the wall stopped and immediately said, "That wall is terribly out of plumb!"

A third day they went down the street together. Again the man who the first day saw nothing wrong with the wall let his glance fall upon it and immediately said: "I believe that wall is going to fall down. It ought to be reported to the authorities."

Every time he looked at the wall, expecting to see the flaw, it appeared worse and worse.

The "new freedom."—Undoubtedly young people are showing more and more a tendency to disregard conventions in the belief that they are not of present-day value. Do you believe they are really misbehaving more than their fathers did, or is their misbehavior simply more conspicuous? How is the "new freedom" of young people working out in the lives of your friends? Christian conferences of young people and institutes where they gather to study ways of serving the church and humanity are crowded with serious students. But so are the places of questionable amusement. Which influence has the upper hand in your school, in your church, in the group of your friends?

The abdication of parents.—In the words of one young man, "Our parents have passed the buck to us." A generation ago the rearing of children was a matter for serious and constant thought, not to speak of prayer; and the rearing of a child was not considered complete until his twenty-first birthday. To-day a great many parents are too busy amusing themselves to pay much attention to the children. Besides, they honestly believe that the child should be allowed to direct his own development, to build up his own "inhibitions" instead of being afflicted with "prohibitions." No fact in modern life is a greater appeal to the honor of young people. The authority exerted over them is very slight; the confidence reposed in them is sublime. It is an altered situation, with new and strange responsibilities.

What we owe to young people as a group.—Young men and young women who feel that they know something

of the responsibility of youth to-day and who have the
advantage of proper home training and associations in
the church should realize that one of their most pressing
debts is to their fellow citizens in their own age group.
The appeal of gamblers, of the producers of perverted
fiction and drama, and of the perverters of sport is directed
to youth. Many young people with ample spending money
and with their power for good or evil increased by public-
school education nevertheless have had very little training
in manners or morals at home. In other countries they
would be suppressed peasants, hopeless of the future and
bound down to unrelieved labor; in this country they are
exhilarated by their privileges and they misbehave. But
many of them at heart are good. For the stability of
Christian America they should be captured. Do you know
personally any such young people? How do you think
they can be made acquainted with the principles you believe lie at the foundation of a strong and happy nation?
How far do they learn these things in the schools? What
is the best way to bring them into the church? Is it not
possible that the very study of the problems confronting
the nation will make an appeal to their better natures?

PROBLEMS OF YOUTH

The problem of alcohol.—There is of course the
problem of how youth may find its own place in the
modern world. The solution of this problem is the great
adventure. There are the problems of physical, mental,
and moral efficiency, and these are personal problems.
There is the problem of youth as a citizen. *The greatest
part of this problem to-day is the problem of alcohol.* Too
many of our people fail to realize that the immensity of
this problem puts it in a class by itself. Its social and
economic implications touch every phase of life. The
solution of this problem will contribute more to social welfare than the solution of any other problem of our day.
And here enters a new responsibility for our Christian
young people and their parents; for the duty of solving
this problem lies upon the church.

A destructive influence.—The America we have known
and loved, the America that has been handed down to

us as a precious heritage from the fathers of early colonial days, the America that represents the product of the labors and sufferings of the men who blazed a trail in the wilderness, endured incredible hardships with stern fortitude, planted the schoolhouse and the church at every frontier crossroad, drove their covered wagons to the Pacific Coast and extended our domain from sea to sea, is ours now to preserve or to lose. There are groups of sincere people who believe that the principles that have heretofore entered into the making of America are worse than useless, that they are the remains of a sterile Puritanism that must be eliminated from American life before we can have an art, a literature, or a society worth while. These groups are trying to break the influence of the churches, to change the methods of education, to destroy the American conception of morality. Above all, they are intent upon overthrowing prohibition, which they consider the perfect flower of the Puritan idea. Youth must decide as to which contending force shall receive the reward of its favor.

What we owe to society.—We owe more to society today than any generation of the past. Our increased opportunities, the infinite gain in wealth and comforts, have come to us under the protection of our social organization. Without the administration of law none of it could have been. We owe a debt of gratitude to the republic that has showered us with so many benefits. What does law mean to our everyday life? Do the taxes we pay yield anything except protection and sanitary facilities?

The Responsibility of the Church

Ancient enemies.—The church is primarily responsible for prohibition, and this responsibility falls particularly upon the Methodist Episcopal Church. In the words of the *Brewers' Journal* of June 1, 1910:

Undoubtedly the church and the saloon originated in prehistoric times—probably simultaneously. And they have been rivals ever since. Man first began to pray to his idols. The priest gathered around him under his sacred tree or in his sanctified cave those whom he could induce to believe in the "gods," while the preparer of the *real* joys of life required no argument to induce people to trade with him. So the saloon man had the advantage from the start. And he has ever maintained it, as is shown by the expenditures for drink as compared with the income of the religious establishment. No wonder that the clergyman feels sore when he contemplates the national drink bill and then looks at the rather insignificant figures representing the sum of "offerings," salary, and appurtenances with which he keeps his business going. The struggle of the church against the "worldly" enjoyments of man is a losing cause, as its champions fight with spiritual weapons against substantial matters.

And the *Brewer and Malster* of June 15, 1912, reveals this same spirit of bitter hatred when it refers to "the Anglo-American churches—those hotbeds of narrow-mindedness and fanaticism." While we spurn the suggestion that this natural hostility between the church and liquor trade arose from selfish considerations on the part of the preacher, we acknowledge with pride that it has long existed; and no church has been more ready to accept the gage of battle than Methodism. Secretary Debar, of the National Wholesale Liquor Dealers' Association, in 1914, said:

> It is only necessary to read the list of those preachers who are active in the present propaganda for legislative prohibition to realize that it is the Methodist Church which is obsessed with the ambition to gain control of our government. This is the fanatical, aggressive, and sometimes unscrupulous force which is leading the movement for political supremacy under the guise of moral reform.

In the same year, October 25, *Bonfort's Wine and Spirit Circular,* evidently having all the branches of Methodism in mind, declared: "We must realize that the entire Methodist Church, with 42,849 ministers and 6,905,095 members, is a solidified, active, aggressive, and obedient unit in this warfare on our trade."

THE ERA OF NATIONAL PROHIBITION

The method that is being tried.—Federal constitutional prohibition has now been in effect for several years. Conditions are radically different from what they were before the policy was adopted. We have forgotten many of the circumstances tending to bring about congressional approval of prohibition. The saloon is a vague memory.

The liquor industry as it existed has been replaced by a trade different in character. People are confused by conflicting claims as to the benefits and failures of the law. It is well to review the subject; to assess the advantages or disadvantages of the policy which has been tried; to ascertain whether the enforcement of prohibition is moving forward to comparative success or is being proved hopeless.

An extreme measure.—The friends of prohibition do not dispute the fact that it is an extreme measure. While no attempt is made to prohibit a man from drinking, it is true that the suppression of the trade makes it difficult for him to obtain the beverage he desires. And when this difficulty becomes greater than his desire for drink, it is in practice, though not in theory, a curtailment of his "personal liberty." Thomas Jefferson said that the best government governed the least. It is therefore necessary to prove that the legalized liquor trade is an evil so hurtful to the common good in its physiological, social, economic, and political effects that the extreme measure of prohibition is a justifiable means of protecting society as a whole, even though some members of society may thereby be inconvenienced. It is necessary to suppress crime. It is necessary to suppress the trade in narcotic drugs except for medicinal purposes. It is also, we believe, necessary to suppress the trade in the narcotic drug alcohol.

A debt to the world.—We should also remember that we, of all people, owe a debt to the world. The boundless resources of our land, the fact that our government is unhampered by traditions that have throttled moral growth in many other countries, enlarge this debt. Few American young people realize the enormous difference in the material wealth of America and the remainder of the world. The Egyptian Arab frequently lives in a hole in the ground. Great masses of people in China look out upon a country denuded of trees, devoid of all beauty, and incapable of producing more than the barest living for the swarming population. The European peasant lives upon black bread and cabbage soup, and his supreme desire is for an opportunity to slip away and get to America. There are far more automobiles in America than in all the remainder of the world, far more telephones. The American table is loaded with fruits from semitropical climes, with vegetables out of season, with an abundance of the staples of life. In no other country is this true. In England the per-capita expenditure for beer is twice the expenditure for milk. The London cockney lives on bread and beer. America has the right and the duty to point the way to the remainder of the world in the proper solution of those social problems which affect so directly the happiness of the average man. We have a great deal to learn from the Orient and from Europe, but it is our privilege in return to carry a message of peace and right-eousness throughout the world. In this series of lessons we are going to examine this greatest social problem in order to find, if possible, the answer this generation should give to the question, What shall we do with the alcohol menace?

QUESTIONS FOR DISCUSSION

Among the young men and women of school age of your acquaintance how far is the new responsibility of youth being used wisely? Where should parental pro-hibitions end, and dependence on the intelligence and the conscience of young people begin?

Specify in what ways the older men and women of your acquaintance behave just about as the young people do. Is this good or bad?

What is valuable in the social customs and traditions handed down from early American life? What answer shall we make to those who say we have outgrown these stand-ards and should not continue to uphold them?

What groups in America are consciously hostile to the preservation of these customs and traditions? Do you know any of these people yourself? Do you know any of them who believe in prohibition? any of them who are Methodists?

Why is our debt to society and to the government greater than that of our parents? What is the influence of machinery on spiritual life and on morals?

Are stimulating amusements a good or bad thing for spirituality? If good, how far are they good?

What is probably the greatest of the social problems in the world to-day? Do your acquaintances generally consider it a social problem or a personal matter?

Why is the church naturally hostile to the legal or illegal traffic in alcoholic beverages? What is your answer to the assertion that the church has no right to express this hostility politically, as that would be "union of church and state"?

Why are Methodists under a particular obligation to understand the liquor problem?

Do you believe that the support of the liquor traffic by patronage or friendship is sinful or merely antisocial? If antisocial, why not also sinful?

What is the broad justification of such an extreme measure as prohibition as applied to the liquor traffic?

Wine is a mocker, strong drink a brawler;
And whosoever erreth thereby is not wise. (Prov. 20. 1.)

It is not for kings, O Lemuel, it is not for kings to drink
   wine;
Nor for princes *to say*, Where is strong drink? (Prov. 31. 4.)

But they said, We will drink no wine; for Jonadab the son
of Rechab, our father, commanded us, saying, Ye shall drink
no wine, neither ye, not your sons, for ever. (Jer. 35. 6.)

CHAPTER II

ALCOHOL THE MOCKER

"And they fling him hour by hour,
  Limbs of men to give him power;
Brains of men to give him cunning;
  And, for dainties to devour,
Children's souls, the little worth;
  Hearts of women cheaply bought.
He takes them and he breaks them
  But he gives them scanty thought."
  —*William Vaughan Moody in "The Brute."*

WHAT is this commodity that is causing so much animated debate, so much social disturbance, throughout the world? Many of us believe that everything has been put in the world for some good purpose. It is hard for a Christian to dissent, however, from the statement that any beverage use of alcohol, and not merely the abuse of it, is to be deplored. What is the proper use of alcohol? To know this we must know just what it is. Alcohol is a habit-forming, irritant, narcotic, depressant drug. It is useful for many mechanical, pharmaceutical, and scientific purposes. Ethyl alcohol is that found in the ordinary alcoholic beverages, such as beer, wine, and whisky. Other alcohols, not usable for beverage purposes, are methyl, or wood alcohol; propylic, butylic, and amylic.

ALCOHOL AND ITS CHARACTERISTICS

How alcohol is produced.—Ethyl alcohol is produced through the decomposition of vegetable or animal matter by the alcohol ferment. This is a minute living organism, capable of assimilating food, eliminating waste products, growing, and multiplying. Alcohol is a waste product, or excretion, of this organism. When the proportion of alcohol in a fermented liquor becomes 13.5 per cent, the ferment is poisoned. Stronger liquors can only be produced by distillation or "fortification." Ethyl alcohol is colorless and has a burning taste.

17

A peculiar drug.—The alcohol ferment is peculiarly interesting because it exists on the very border line separating the animal and vegetable kingdoms. It is sensitive to heat and cold; even susceptible to disease, although remarkably tenacious of life. But it multiplies by budding. A new cell sprouts from an old one and, by the development of granules liberated by the bursting of the mother cell, becomes the nucleus of still other cells. Its multiplication is especially rapid in the presence of sugar.

A queer argument.—Some enemies of prohibition have contended that since fruit juices will ferment if left alone, the whole argument against the consumption of alcohol becomes absurd. They say, "Who can be held responsible for this natural fermentation?" and "Since it is natural, why should it not be used?" Practically everything else to be found in the pantry will also ferment or decay; but when in any other substance this process has taken place, we consider it unfit for food.

"Wine is a mocker."—The word of Solomon arraigning wine as a mocker, or, as we might freely translate, a deceiver, and strong drink as a raging "brawler," has never been surpassed as a definition of the character of alcohol. We are interested in knowing just what are the properties of this product that has played such a large part in history.

Alcohol a poison.—First, let us understand that it is a poison. "Intoxicating" really means "poisonous," as any druggist will testify if he notices the significance of the syllable "toxic." This poison has a peculiar affinity for the more important cells of the body. In all its effects it is the direct negation of water. While both are colorless, it will be noticed that

WATER	ALCOHOL
Will not burn.	Burns easily.
Has no taste.	Has burning taste.
Cools and refreshes the skin.	Burns and inflames the skin.
Is necessary to healthy life.	Is unnecessary to healthy life.
Makes a seed grow.	Kills the seed.
Softens all foods.	Hardens all foods.
Is itself a food.	Is a poison.
Will not dissolve resin.	Easily dissolves resin.
Does not intoxicate.	Intoxicates.
Benefits the body.	Injures the body.

Is a constituent of every living body cell.	Is not a constituent of any living body cell.
Aids decomposition.	Prevents decomposition.
Quenches thirst.	Creates thirst.

Alcohol is not a food. At every point it is different in its nature from foods:

FOOD	ALCOHOL
The same quantity produces the same effect.	More and more is required to produce a given effect upon a person.
Its habitual use does not produce a desire for more in ever-increasing amounts.	Its habitual use is likely to induce an uncontrollable desire for more in ever-increasing quantities.
All foods are oxidized slowly.	Alcohol is oxidized rapidly.
All foods are stored in the body.	Alcohol is not stored in the body.
Foods are wholesome and beneficial to the healthy body; they may injure the body in certain phases of disease.	Alcohol is a poisonous excretion, which may be beneficial in certain cases of diseases (though physicians use it far less than formerly, and many do not use it at all), but is never beneficial to the healthy body.
The young are advised to take plenty of food.	The young are always advised to abstain from alcohol.
The use of foods is not followed by reaction.	The use of alcohol, as of narcotics in general, is followed by a reaction.
The use of foods is followed by an increase in the activity of the muscles and brain cells.	The use of alcohol is followed by a decrease in the activity of the muscles and brain cells.

Alcohol is a food for the ferment of acetic acid, or vinegar, and is a poison for everything else. There is very little scientific opposition to this statement at the present time.

Some simple demonstrations.—The essential differences between alcohol and water are easily demonstrated by the following simple experiments:

Add water to sugar and salt in separate vessels. These things at once dissolve.

Add alcohol to sugar and salt in another separate vessel. No solution occurs.

Pour a saturated solution of salt and water into a test
tube; then a drop or two of alcohol. The salt is thrown out
of solution.

Add water to bread in a cup. The bread is reduced to a
sop or pap. Add alcohol to bread. No change occurs. Bread,
sugar, meat, fruits, fish, and, indeed, all foods may be indefinitely preserved in alcohol.

Add water to camphor in a tube. There is no action. Add
alcohol to camphor in a tube and warm it. It dissolves, and
you form a perfume. Add water to the dissolved camphor.
It is thrown out of solution again.

Add water to resin in a tube. No action occurs. Add
alcohol to resin in a tube and warm it. The resin dissolves,
and you form a varnish. Add water to the dissolved resin.
It is thrown out of solution.

Revealing experiments.—The following experiments
show that alcohol is not a food and that it is injurious to
living organisms:

Procure two goldfish. Put one in pure water and one in
water containing about two per cent of alcohol. The latter
will die within a day or two.

If you fill one glass with beer and put into another one
twentieth as much milk, the two quantities will have equal
nutritive value. You will have an ocular demonstration that
milk is twenty times as nourishing as beer, nor does it contain the poison to be found in beer.

Questions to think about.—What are some of the facts
brought out by these demonstrations, which may run
counter to the opinions of your own family and associates
in times past? Is there any reason why we should hold
to the belief in the value of alcohol for internal consumption because our grandmothers believed in it? Do
the facts here established warrant the conclusion that
drunkenness is the only evil resulting from the use of
intoxicating liquors?

The "Food" Value of Alcohol

A drug, not a food.—Alcohol has practically no food
value. When taken into the body it is rapidly utilized
as a temporary food, being partially burned as a fuel and
causing body heat, but this effect is almost infinitesimal.
As Sir Spencer Wells, M.D., F.R.S., said, "We must regard alcohol as a drug, and not as a food." Dr. Harvey
W. Wiley, former chief chemist of the United States,

stated the fact in his clear way as follows: "It is without question a substance which does not nourish the body, build tissue, or repair waste."

"Liquid bread."—Beer has been called "liquid bread," but it has only about four per cent of nutritive material. The amount of poison in beer exceeds its food value. The statement "Beer is liquid bread" is frequently attributed to the famous German chemist Baron Von Liebig but it cannot be located in any of Von Liebig's scientific works, and in Letter VI of his "Letters on Chemistry," to be found on page 22 of his *Complete Works on Chemistry,* he says: "Beer, wine, and spirits furnish no elements capable of entering into the composition of the blood, muscular fiber, or any part that is a vital principle." And he says: "Nine quarts of the best ale contain as much nourishment as would lie on the end of a table knife." And still again: "If man drinks daily eight or ten quarts of the best Bavarian beer, in the course of twelve months he will have taken into his stomach the nutritive constituents of a five-pound loaf of bread."

Flour versus beer.—Professor G. O. Higley, while with the Department of Chemistry of Ohio Wesleyan University, published an elaborate study of the food value of flour and of beer. He found the ratio of proteids in beer to those in flour as 1 to 80, of carbohydrates as 1 to 61, and of fats as .0 to 0.28. To furnish a hard-working man with the amount of protein needed each day it would be necessary to give him 108 glasses of beer, costing $5.40, as compared with 37.9 ounces of flour, costing 6.8 cents. To supply him with the carbohydrates needed for his daily ration it would be necessary to give him 52 glasses of beer, costing $2.60, or flour costing 4.3 cents. The same money expended for beer and flour would yield 94.05 calories in the case of beer and 2,785.84 calories in the case of flour. The calorie is the unit of measure of nutritive value. Professor Higley made a similar comparison between milk and beer with similar conclusions.

Is Alcohol a Good Medicine?

Becoming obsolete.—Twenty-five years ago not one physician in ten condemned the use of alcohol as an in-

ternal medicine. Whisky, wine, and beer were prescribed
in medical practice in quantities equal to the quantities
used in moderate drinking. About the opening of this
century, however, eminent physicians in both Europe and
America began to advocate the limitation of the use of alcohol as a medicine and to condemn its use as a beverage,
so that in 1912 the *London Times* said, "According to recent developments of scientific opinion it is not impossible
that a belief in the strengthening and the supporting qualities of alcohol will eventually become as obsolete as a belief in witchcraft." An inquiry directed by Dr. Winfield
Scott Hall, at that time of Northwestern University, to
forty-two hospitals revealed that in thirty-nine of them
the decrease in the use of alcohol as a medicine had been so
great that practically none was used. Replies from presi-
dents of State medical associations and from city health
officers revealed a similar state of affiairs.

Similarly the common use of alcohol as a household
remedy has steadily declined as popular intelligence concerning its real effects has increased. Concerning this
Captain Richard P. Hobson says:

The greater liability to disease in drinkers is true as to
pneumonia, typhoid, and, broadly speaking, to all diseases.
So the idea that you need alcohol, or that it is a legitimate
household remedy, has been entirely exploded. Henceforth,
I believe, when laws are drafted for the various States,
legislators will not make any exception to the use of alcohol,
or alcoholic beverages, even for use for medicinal purposes.
You can wipe out its use for medicinal purposes without loss.

Not a stimulant.—In *Hare's Practical Therapeutics*
(edition of 1916), a textbook on every physician's shelves,
by Dr. Robert A. Hare, professor of therapeutics of the
Jefferson Medical College of Philadelphia, we find the following:

Alcohol never acts as a stimulant to the brain, the spinal
cord, or the nerves. The increased activity of thought and
speech is not due to stimulation but to depression of the
inhibitory nervous apparatus. The activity is, therefore, that
caused by lack of control and is not a real increase of energy.

On this point there is an almost unlimited amount of
medical testimony. Dr. Henry S. Williams says:

The traditional rôle of alcohol is that of a stimulant. It has been supposed to stimulate digestion and assimilation; to stimulate the heart's action; to stimulate muscular activity and strength; to stimulate the mind. The new evidence seems to show that, in the final analysis, alcohol stimulates none of these activities; that its final effect is everywhere depressive and inhibitory (at any rate as regards higher functions) rather than stimulative; that, in short, it is properly to be classed with the anesthetics and narcotics.

"More harm than good."—The overwhelming weight of medical opinion seems to be that alcohol is not a preventive of pneumonia, that it is not useful in treating tuberculosis, that it is not even good for snake bite nor sunstroke. Dr. W. A. Evans, the well-known medical editor of the *Chicago Tribune,* has said, "A sunstroke is often nothing more nor less than a beer stroke," and again, "In cases of shock whisky does more harm than good." The *Journal of the American Medical Association* has said, "The light of exact investigation has shown that the therapeutic value of alcohol rests on an insecure basis." And Dr. Reid Hunt, famous physician of the Public Health Marine Hospital Service, has declared, "The field of usefulness of alcohol in therapeutics positively does not exist at all." Testimony of this character could be extended indefinitely; but suffice it to say that if one is tempted to use rock-and-rye to head off a bad cold, the best physicians in the world will tell him he is doing the worst possible thing.

As the conclusion of an article on "Alcohol and the Individual," Dr. Henry S. Williams, quoted above, says:

So I am bound to believe, on the evidence, that if you take alcohol habitually, in any quantity whatever, it is to some extent a menace to you. I am bound to believe, in the light of what science has revealed: (1) that you are tangibly threatening the physical structures of your stomach, your liver, your kidneys, your heart, your blood-vessels, your nerves, your brain; (2) that you are unequivocally decreasing your capacity for work in any field be it physical, intellectual, or artistic; (3) that you are in some measure lowering the grade of your mind, dulling your higher æsthetic sense, and taking the finer edge off your morals; (4) that you are distinctly lessening your chances of maintaining health and attaining longevity; and (5) that you may be entailing upon your descendants yet unborn a bond of incalculable misery.

The Right Use of Alcohol

External use.—Has alcohol, then, no medical value? As a refrigerant to cool fevered bodies, as a solvent of drugs (for which purpose it is unequaled), and as a rub for tired muscles alcohol is invaluable.

Industrial uses.—Its greatest field of usefulness, however, is in industry. It is absolutely indispensable in the preparation of silk, in the making of felt hats, and in the compounding of perfumes and toilet waters. Without it the varnish trade would languish, and even the maker of hairbrushes would be sorely inconvenienced. When our gasoline supply is exhausted, we shall simply construct engines with greater compression and use alcohol made from cheap potatoes and farm refuse. Alcohol is not only good: it is a mighty servant of man; but God never intended it for use as a beverage.

Controlling a good servant.—A great many practical problems arise from the numerous proper uses of alcohol. If it is a commodity so useful for trade and in everyday life, how is it to be controlled and still remain available for useful purposes? Do you think that the government should itself produce all of the alcohol used or should it leave it to private industry? Is alcohol a greater blessing than evil under the conditions of prohibition? Do you make any use of it yourself? If so, how? The problem of temperance is a problem of alcoholism, and the cause of alcoholism is alcohol. Prohibition is needed, however, not simply as an effective method of dealing with alcoholism, but also with certain social and economic problems not directly connected with the worst phases of alcoholism. These we shall discuss later.

Questions for Discussion

Can you name any natural substance that has no use?

What is the parallel between the process of fermentation and that of decay?

Is alcohol a poison in the sense that prussic acid is a poison? If it is different, how?

Alcohol looks like water: what are the differences?

What are the differences between food and alcohol?

How does the fact that alcohol precipitates solutions affect digestion?

Alcohol dissolves many substances: how is it useful in industrial life?

What are the food qualities of beer?

Do you personally know anyone who thinks that beer has food value? What were his antecedents and training?

Is alcohol good for a cold? for a snake bite? for prostration?

If not, why is it that our parents frequently believe it good for the treatment of these ills?

In just how many ways do you find alcohol useful in your home?

How should the country make alcohol available to you for legitimate purposes and still restrain its consumption as a beverage?

Who hath woe? who hath sorrow? who hath contentions?
Who hath complaining? who hath wounds without cause?
Who hath redness of eyes?
They that tarry long at the wine;
They that go to seek out mixed wine.
Look not thou upon the wine when it is red.
When it sparkleth in the cup,
When it goeth down smoothly:
At the last it biteth like a serpent,
And stingeth like an adder.   (Prov. 23. 29-32.)

CHAPTER III

HOW ALCOHOL SUBDUED THE RACE

The truth is, in my opinion, that the consumption of alcohol is kept up by tradition, by the assumption that so prevalent a practice must have virtues, by the fear of individuals to break away from custom, and by the well-known difficulty of emancipating oneself from drug habits.—*Professor Irving Fisher, Yale University.*

ALCOHOL was probably discovered at the beginning of the agricultural age, or thirty thousand years ago. It may even be that the first man who made a vessel that would contain liquids crushed his wild grapes in order to drink the juice. Perhaps he left some of his grape juice while absent for some days on a hunting trip and on returning, found that it had acquired a new and peculiar flavor. Who the first "drunk" was we do not know, but we do know that it was so long ago that he was probably a wretched, skin-clad savage, tortured by hunger and thirst, oppressed by cold, and hunted by animals. There is in mankind a natural desire for stimulation, for the power of complete abandonment, for the "obliteration of a part of the field of consciousness." How joyously, then, this savage must have welcomed the discovery of a drug that would temporarily deaden the pangs of his cruel life, which would even make him feel like a god, exalting his ego and suppressing all memory of his weakness and sorrow! The barbarian soon came to consider alcohol essential to the proper observance of worship, the ceremony of marriages, funerals, dances, preparations for war, and celebrations of victory. "About its use," says Partridge, "crystallized myth and superstition, rite and ceremony, in endless variety." How much of this is held over to more civilized times! And how much less excusable it is now, in this age of highly developed music and play!

Barbarous people have always induced excitement as a means of divine worship and as a part of ceremony by violent dancing, by drugs, even by self-torture. Epilepsy, chorea, and other neurotic conditions are voluntarily sought by many savage tribes as a means of reaching that desired moment of utter abandonment. In modern times the saloon became the agency of this impulse toward exhilaration. In the words of Warner modern man "seeks a means of escaping from monotony and suffering; he desires to forget his aches and pains, his sorrow and trouble, and he does not hesitate to use external and artificial agents when they will serve that end." In this connection it is of the highest importance to realize the truth of Samuelsson's statement that prevalence of intoxication marks two periods in the history of a race: the period preceding the highest cultural development and the period of degeneracy. The barbarian or the degenerate thinks he must release his soul by drugs; the truly cultivated man finds release in the power of his mind and spirit.

ALCOHOL IN CIVILIZATION

The literature of Egypt, Babylonia, and Canaan shows that drunkenness was common among those people who knew only how to produce wine and barley beer. Egyptian frescoes on temples tell the story of beer-brewing many thousands of years ago. We even find that one early fanatic deplored the growth of the industry and wanted it at least partially suppressed. The Egyptian beverage of which Herodotus writes was beer, and the art of making it was attributed to Isis. In the Orient there were periods of heavy drinking. In the barbaric stage of early Europe we find our Teutonic forefathers sodden with alcohol. The Norsemen conceived of heaven as a place where the days were spent in hunting, and the nights in drunken revels. Gin came near being the destruction of eighteenth-century England. "Retailers of intoxicants," says Lecky, "put out signs announcing that their customers could become drunk for a penny, dead drunk for twopence, and have straw on which to lie for nothing."

WHY MEN DRINK

The motive of escape.—Civilized man, like his barbarian ancestor, sometimes seeks escape from life. There is undoubtedly a natural impulse to seek stimulation of the physical powers. There is also an impulse to seek release from all of the conventions that restrict conduct and thought. If anything the latter motive becomes stronger as civilization progresses; for, after all, civilization is imposed upon nature. Deep within all of us lie remnants of savage impulses and motives. We feel that civilization is becoming too much for us and we wish to revert to more primitive habits and needs of life in order to find relief from conditions of high pressure. We feel that if we can suppress the higher impulses that are the product of civilization we shall find relaxation, recreation, relief from responsibility, rest from toil, the illusion of a happier world. We long to turn back the clock of time. These facts, however, should not cause us to jump to the conclusion that the consumption of alcohol is justified by these desires of ancient and modern man; for we may find a release from inhibitions and a legitimate revel in illusions in the beautiful stimulation of music, in dramatic expression, in the varied forms of play which are now available to the whole American population. The so-called intoxication impulse is really unnatural. It is perversion of a natural impulse to seek mental release and physical expression in healthful ways. Why should the attention of Christian people turn more definitely toward the problem of play? How is it linked with the problem of alcoholism and the liquor traffic? What reasons have you for thinking that the playground and the fine arts can be made to take the place in the hearts of children and young people once occupied by cruder forms of pleasure?

The social motive.—People like to see an entertainment in company with their friends. They wish to play surrounded by others of similar age and tastes. The normal man desires to take most of his pleasures as one of a group and thus make himself a part of the life of others. We have noticed how the use of alcohol took on so many ceremonial aspects in tribal life. The savage drank to beastly drunkenness but he drank seldom and socially. In civilized life also the social motive has been one of the chief supports of the liquor trade. Solitary drinking is even now exceptional. In Rome and Greece alcohol was consumed at feasts. In the destroyed city of Herculaneum more than nine hundred public drinking houses were found. The Germanic peoples consumed their liquors at great drinking banquets. In early Anglo-Saxon life the trade union, or guild, developed from the meetings of workmen at the alehouse. Literary men met and gossiped in public houses, and the social traditions of alcohol became an influence. The colonists who founded our own country had shared in this evil social heritage. Drink must be there when the baby was baptized or the church dedicated. Its blight was present at weddings. It welcomed the guest and sped his departure. Farmers gave it freely to their "hands," and wherever there was a barn raising, a logrolling, a dance, or even a funeral, "it was respectable not merely to drink but to get gloriously drunk." Even to-day it persists with many people who naïvely think one crude or foolish if he refuses the before-dinner cocktail.

THE SALOON IN AMERICA

The mission of the saloon.—Wicked as the saloon was, some things could be said for it. It was logically conceived. The commodity offered by the saloon afforded an unnatural satisfaction of a natural physical craving for a stimulation of the primary senses and a suppression of the inhibitory influences of civilization. It is a significant thing that even to-day, after thousands of years of drinking, the appetite for alcohol itself must be created in every drinker. We often say that some child has "inherited" an appetite for alcohol. Authoritative opinion, however, is that no such appetite is ever inherited. The weaknesses of mind and body which made the father peculiarly susceptible to the bad effects of alcohol are no doubt present in the child, but no child likes the taste of alcohol. The saloon as an institution for creating the alcohol appetite was very nearly perfect. It offered not simply an appeal to the physical impulse but was in every sense of the word a social agency, tending to establish liquor drinking as a social custom and tradition. Here man met his fellow man in democratic contact. Here might be found tables for political, fraternal, and social

conferences. Here were all facilities for the playing of
cards or other games. Here were small sandwiches to be
had free of charge by the man who was hungry enough to
want "just a bite" and not hungry enough to want to go to
a restaurant. Here were comfort facilities of every kind.
It was the place where a man who had fallen down on a
rainy day might wash his muddy hands and might have
his clothes brushed and his shoes shined. Here he got
reports, inning by inning, of baseball games. Here he
found all the news and discussion of legitimate and illegal sporting events. Here, if he thought he *had* to
have a fight he was afforded the opportunity in a remote
room. The saloon was a social institution and made a
social appeal. Not the least of its appeals was the fact
that in this country it was distinctly a man's institution,
a place of retreat from family cares.

Has the saloon left a void?—In the last days before
prohibition social workers raised the question "If you
close the saloon, what will take its place?" and they contended that substitutes must be provided. Prohibitionists
answered that men resented being taken care of, as if
they were children, and declared that they must themselves, by the expression of a demand, create the institution
or institutions that would meet the need of a democratic
social center. How, in your own community, has this
need been met, or *has* it been met? In many communities
men who formerly found fretful wives and bickering
children insupportable, after prohibition found their
homes strangely attractive. When their wives were relieved of worry on account of insufficient funds for housekeeping purposes; when the whining of the children was
silenced by an ample supply of milk, butter, and fresh
fruit; when a victrola was added to the household
equipment, and the eldest boy was allowed to tinker
with a radio, no refuge from home unhappiness was
needed. We have found that the saloon had a social
mission largely because the home was being prevented
by the saloon from fulfilling its own mission. Men gather
now in the cheap restaurants and in clubrooms for the
conferences that formerly took place in the saloon. The
hotels of necessity have been forced to offer the emergency

comfort conveniences formerly offered by the saloon and
have seen themselves compensated by the readiness of the
public to pay small fees, to patronize the adjoining barber
shop and shoe-shining stands, and to be generous with
tips. The nickel-in-the-slot piano of the saloon has been
replaced by free band concerts in the parks, by free radio
concerts, and by motion-picture houses, which offer to
the casual seeker of amusement, to the transient,
and both to the former saloon customer and his wife ready
and cheap entertainment. Every corner drug store, every
cigar stand, has a soda fountain, and men by the millions
are using them—men who formerly sought the saloon for
refreshment. Baseball reports even while the games are
being played come over every radio. Playgrounds for
adults as well as for children have multiplied. Ten
times as many people are playing golf as ever played before, and in many cities municipal links put the game far
below the luxury class. The saloon was coining money
by catering in a perverted way to normal, natural demands, and these demands to-day are being healthfully
met by a score of social agencies that could never have
prospered before prohibition.

The saloon in business.—The saloon keeper, however,
was not in business simply to fill a social need; he was in
business to make money. The first impulse of every business man is to increase trade; for every sale means profits,
and the profits increase rapidly after the overhead charges
have been cared for. Especially in America the business
man does not wait for trade to come to him; he goes into
the highways and byways and finds it. It was the business of the saloon keeper to create a liquor appetite and
for profit to satisfy that appetite. So every American
citizen became familiar with the slogan "The beer that
made Milwaukee famous," and every man, woman, and
child in our cities was constantly told by the colored
billboards and the flashing brilliance of electric lights that
"beer is liquid bread," that it "strengthens the aged and
nourishes growing children," that it is a "temperance"
drink. Newspapers carried many millions of dollars'
worth of this advertising. The saloons were always
located on the busiest corners in the cities, and attractive

displays in the show windows called trade from the streets. All the devices of modern trade promotion were developed to the highest point in support of the liquor business. The last few years before prohibition this urgent trade promotion took on particularly vicious forms. Whisky mail-order houses arose like mushrooms in cities, and millions of circulars were carried by the United States mail into all prohibition territory. Sometimes these circulars did not even bear a name as part of the letterhead. One house advertised a brand known as "Post Office Whisky," and the trade-mark bore a picture of Uncle Sam. Another house offered a combination bargain consisting of a box of cigars, a quart of whisky, and a revolver all for $3.59. Crimes of the most horrible character were directly traceable to the consumption of whisky thus advertised and distributed. Congress never did a more creditable thing than when it prohibited the transmission of liquor advertising through the mails and stopped the iniquitous mail-order business in whisky.

Politics and the saloon.—But another motive entered into the strengthening of the saloon as an institution. In 1862 the federal government first accepted revenue from the sale of liquors. "The liquor business was weak when the license system was introduced, but under the fostering care of this accursed fraud it has become the autocrat of politics," declared John B. Finch in bitter indignation. "The acceptance of federal revenue from the liquor business was in itself the immediate cause of aggressive commercial expansion of the traffic, multiplied attractions to entice men into saloons, the careful fostering of the drink habit as a trade asset, and a comprehensive, far-reaching educational propaganda to offset the activities of temperance organizations, especially where such a propaganda would result with the greatest ease in an extension of the drinking custom." But more important was the fact that the acceptance of this revenue marked a revolution in the relations of the state and the trade. For the first time the federal government was obligated by the acceptance of money to assist alcohol in "subduing the race." The federal receipt for revenue meant that the holder, given permission within the limits of existing restrictive legislation to carry

on his business, was afforded the protection of all the
government machinery and was allowed to make use of
all the means at his command to promote the liquor industry.   The inevitable result was that corrupt politics
entered into an alliance with the saloon.   It quickly became the natural resort and agency of the grafter.   The
saloon paid untold millions for political protection because
without political protection its position would have been
intolerable if not impossible.   There was one way, and
only one, in which to destroy the political evils of the
saloon, and that was to destroy the entire license system
that supported those evils.

The Theory of Prohibition

Damming a stream.—At bottom the theory of prohibition is that the law should make it easy for men to
do that which is socially right, and hard to do that which
is socially wrong.   The law should be an influence in the
community for protecting the common welfare, for im-
proving the general health, for increasing the general
prosperity.   There may have been a time in civilization
or before civilization when the beverage use of alcohol and
the trade in alcohol contributed to the happiness of the
race.   We believe that such a time, if it ever existed, has
passed.   If you erect a dam across a stream, the stream
immediately begins to seek a new channel.   It may over-
flow the dam at times and may even break down the
barrier, which will have to be reestablished; but eventually
a new channel will be created.   Prohibition has erected a
barrier to the perverted expression of the physical, social,
economic, and political impulses toward stimulation, but
there is no desire to suppress these motives.   The pressure
of law is used to divert the stream into a new channel,
where its flow will be health-giving.

Broadening the channel.—It cannot be said that the
effect of the law is unavailing.   The public place of sale
has been suppressed.   The many institutional characteristics that appealed to the social motive are gone.   The
economic motive that found expression in methods of
trade expansion has been changed to the furtive and
criminal efforts of the bootlegger.   The influence of the

drink traffic in politics has been immensely lessened.
Meanwhile the new channel is being deepened and
broadened, and the vital needs of the oncoming generation
will seek it more and more. Custom and a tradition
are being changed. The event is one of the most pro-
foundly interesting and significant things in modern
history.

QUESTIONS FOR DISCUSSION

What physical need prompted men to seek intoxication?

When you feel such a need yourself, what other ways
do you recognize in which you find the need satisfied?

With what social customs is alcohol identified closely
in your community?

What is your answer to those who maintain that its
use as a beverage serves a social need?

In your opinion was the saloon the worst possible means
of distributing alcoholic liquors?

What good purposes did the saloon serve?

How would the social developments of the past few
years have changed the saloon if it still existed?

Discuss different methods of liquor distribution which
might take the place of the saloon.

How would those methods tend to change under the
pressure of the physical and social motives toward drink?

What reason have we for believing the contemplated
methods of distribution could be freed from the political
and economic motives?

What were some of the direct effects of the introduction
of the license system?

In what ways can the church meet the social need
formerly met by the saloon?

Jesus answered and said unto them, Destroy this temple, and in three days I will raise it up. The Jews therefore said, Forty and six years was this temple in building, and wilt thou raise it up in three days? But he spake of the temple of his body. (John 2. 19-21.)

But Daniel purposed in his heart that he would not defile himself with the king's dainties, nor with the wine which he drank: therefore he requested of the prince of the eunuchs that he might not defile himself. Now God made Daniel to find kindness and compassion in the sight of the prince of the eunuchs. And the prince of the eunuchs said unto Daniel, I fear my lord the king, who hath appointed your food and your drink: for why should he see your faces worse looking than the youths that are of your own age? so would ye endanger my head with the king. Then said Daniel to the steward whom the prince of the eunuchs had appointed over Daniel, Hananiah, Mishael, and Azariah: Prove thy servants, I beseech thee, ten days; and let them give us pulse to eat, and water to drink. Then let our countenances be looked upon before thee, and the countenance of the youths that eat of the king's dainties; and as thou seest, deal with thy servants.

So he hearkened unto them in this matter, and proved them ten days. And at the end of ten days their countenances appeared fairer, and they were fatter in flesh, than all the youths that did eat of the king's dainties. So the steward took away their dainties, and the wine that they should drink, and gave them pulse.

Now as for these four youths, God gave them knowledge and skill in all learning and wisdom: and Daniel had understanding in all visions and dreams. And at the end of the days which the king had appointed for bringing them in, the prince of the eunuchs brought them in before Nebuchadnezzar. And the king communed with them; and among them all was found none like Daniel, Hananiah, Mishael, and Azariah: therefore stood they before the king. And in every matter of wisdom and understanding, concerning which the king inquired of them, he found them ten times better than all the magicians and enchanters that were in all his realm. (Dan. 1. 8-20.)

CHAPTER IV

QUESTIONS THAT MAY ARISE THIS VERY DAY

The basis of intemperance is the effort to secure through drugs the feeling of happiness when happiness does not exist. Men destroy their nervous system for the tingling pleasure they feel as its structures are torn apart.—*Dr. David Starr Jordan, Leland Stanford Jr. University.*

To use liquor is to the nervous system like placing sand in a watch: it wears it out rapidly, making it a worthless, useless thing.—*Luther Burbank.*

A YOUNG college man, just about to leave his room for an important examination, was mentally tired. He hesitated a few moments and then poured out two ounces of whisky and drained the glass. Was he wise or foolish?

A young athlete, playing in the finals he hoped would give him the tennis championship of his city, felt completely exhausted at the conclusion of the second set. He stepped to his bench and, taking out a tiny bottle of brandy, drank it to give him the strength to go through the third set. Did he show good judgment or bad judgment?

A workman, engaged in moving heavy furniture and proud of his strength, boasted that he could place a piano in the wagon by himself. Before attempting the feat he took a pint bottle of whisky from his pocket and took a long drink. Did it help him?

A young woman having just reached home after a street car trip, feeling chilled and "sneezy," went to the medicine cabinet and took a large glass of wine in order to head off possible influenza. Was this a wise use of alcohol?

A miner in Alaska, on the trail and fearing death by freezing, drank whisky to make him warm. A workman on a city street, feeling nearly overcome by the summer heat, drank a bottle of beer to make him cool. Which was right, or were both wrong?

These practical questions of everyday life are readily

answered if we know the physiological reasons for abstinence.

How Alcohol Affects the System

The action of alcohol in the body.—Since alcohol is "an irritant, depressant, narcotic drug," when it enters the body it affects the whole human system but is only slightly absorbed into the blood. It gives every evidence of being an intruder, an unwelcome and hostile visitor to the human system.

What alcohol does to the brain.—Dr. W. A. Chapple, of London, says: "Alcohol is a poison, having a specific affinity for the nerve centers of the brain and paralyzing those centers in the inverse order of their development: the last developed suffering first and most, and the first developed suffering last and least." Affinities are not so rare that this affinity of alcohol for the brain cells is a surprising quality. The poison of lead has a peculiar affinity for the muscles of the wrist, mercury for the salivary glands, manganese for the liver, arsenic for the coating of the stomach, strychnine for the spinal cord; but alcohol is a ready solvent of fat, and to this fact Professor Hans Meyer, of the University of Vienna, attributes its affinity for the cells of the brain, which are composed largely of a fatty substance. The healthy brain cell has a symmetrical center and branches; but under alcohol the centers become irregular, and the branches frayed in appearance. Frequently it is the case that continued drinking so damages the cell that it will not recover, and a damaged brain cell is never replaced. The assertion of Doctor Chapple that alcohol attacks first the higher qualities of the mind is also well established and generally acknowledged. These qualities are based upon brain cells which have been produced during the more recent periods of man's development. They are racially less mature and resistant. "Civilized man equals the brute animal plus the brain development," says the New York Health Department in a bulletin. "Alcohol blots out the high brain development and leaves the brute animal."

Intoxication like insanity.—Common observation indicates clearly the effect of alcohol in reversing the evolu-

tionary processes. The man who becomes intoxicated
loses first his sense of decency, his ability to think clearly
and accurately, and to associate ideas. As his intoxication
progresses it affects those nerve and brain powers which
control the senses. He begins to see double, to be unable
to control his movements; his powers of hearing and sight
are distinctly lessened. It has been well said that intoxication epitomizes the whole history of insanity. The man
who becomes dead drunk within the space of a few hours
undergoes very much the same change as the man who
becomes gradually insane, and he who keeps his association
and motor senses slightly drugged all the time by
"moderate" drinking is not entirely a sane man. He
is constantly drunk to a slight degree and is therefore
constantly insane to a slight degree.

The sign of a weak brain.—The day has passed when
any intelligent and informed person boasts of the ability
to "carry liquor well." Such ability is a sign not of a
strong body but of a weak brain. The brain that is not
sensitive to alcohol is an atavistic product. The cave man
was probably able to "carry liquor well"; Thomas A.
Edison probably would carry it very ill indeed.

Drinking and Thinking

A handicap.—Now for our problem as to the wisdom
of the use of whisky by the young man undertaking the
heavy mental work of a college examination. In the
first place we must recognize the fact that he very soon
felt extremely alert and was sure he was in much better
condition to handle his examinations. "Wine is a mocker."
The fact is (and the fact has been established by scientific
experimentation) that he had further handicapped himself. It is possible that a cup of strong black coffee would
have helped him for a limited time, although it would have
been followed by a distinct reaction. Even a few lumps
of sugar probably would have made some difference. But
the work of Krapelin, Dietel, Vintschgau, Vogt, Stehr,
and many others has demonstrated that alcohol, even in
very small quantities, has a distinctly unfavorable effect
upon the ability to do mental work.

What experiments have shown.—The deleterious effect of

alcohol consumption upon brain work has been established by experiments to determine the effect of alcohol upon the ability of the subject to respond quickly to a flash of light, to determine the effect of alcohol upon the reaction time required to press a right or left telegraph key, upon type-writing, and upon mental tests similar to those now called intelligence tests. One glass of beer will decrease the powers of memory, reason, and perception for a certain length of time; and steady, so-called moderate drinking produces an abiding impairment of the mental capability. Investigations made by Dr. Alfred Stehr, in Germany, disclosed a distinct loss of efficiency on Mondays after the drinking on Sundays among a group of bottle workers in Dresden. This loss amounted to 28.5 per cent.

The Effect of Alcohol Consumption Upon Muscular Power

The tennis player's failure.—Now to return to our young tennis player. Soon after drinking the brandy he felt much better. There seemed to be greater muscular power. Certainly there was more confidence. He began to hit the ball hard, but for some reason his errors multi-plied. In the first two sets he had been placing the ball in the corners with great accuracy. In the third set when he would clear the net, he would find the ball badly off in direction or entirely too long. Once or twice in attempting to stroke the ball he missed it entirely. "Wine is a mocker."

Connie Mack's testimony.—Connie Mack, manager of the Philadelphia Athletics, winner of the world's base-ball championship in 1910, 1911, and 1913, said: "Alcohol is practically eliminated from baseball. I have twenty-five players. Of that number fifteen do not know the taste of liquor." He further says: "Baseball men are not now of the drinking class. It's the survival of the fittest."

What Hugh Fullerton found.—Hugh Fullerton, now with the United Press and one of the leading baseball writers of the United States, in conversation with the Research Secretary of the Board of Temperance, Prohi-bition, and Public Morals of the Methodist Episcopal Church, said:

I was at a training camp in the South in the spring and became interested in a young fellow who seemed to have a bright baseball future. I found him drinking beer one day and warned him that it would send him back to the minors quicker than anything else.

"Oh, a little beer won't hurt me; it's good for me," he said.

I knew better and wanted to prove what I knew, so I took a baseball guide of 1904, made a list of players, and followed them through the successive guides up to 1914.

From the major-league roster of 1904 I selected the names of thirty players who drank intoxicants and thirty who did not drink, choosing only those who were known by me as drinkers or abstainers. I traced each one to see what had become of him. Here is the table:

DRINKERS IN SERVICE

1904	1905	1906	1907	1908	1909	1910	1911	1912	1913	1914
30	26	20	15	9[1]	4	4	2	2	2	2[1]

NONDRINKERS IN SERVICE

1904	1905	1906	1907	1908	1909	1910	1911	1912	1913	1914
30	28	28	24	21	16	12	10	9	9	8

Mind, these men are classed as "drinkers," not drunkards. Not more than four listed as drinkers ever were drunkards. They were "moderate" drinkers. Several of the nondrinkers had occasionally taken a drink but were not drinkers. The others were total abstainers.

The figures interested me so much I investigated as to their present physical and financial welfare. This resulted in another table:

	Drinkers	*Nondrinkers*
Down and out	8	1
Medium	5	9
Prosperous	3[2]	16
Dead	9	2
Unaccounted for	5	2

Most of these statistics in the second table came from either talking with the players or from letters they wrote in reply to my queries. Five of the drinkers responded quickly and asked for a loan.

My investigation did not stop there, however. I took up the matter of batting and I found that the abstainers showed much better records than the drinkers, although the latter class included a few of the great stars of the game who tended to bring up the average greatly.

I have watched this matter of drinking in athletics for a long time, and there are no two sides to it. One of the greatest baseball machines of the present generation was shot to

[1] One quit drinking.
[2] Two of them still in the game.

pieces by beer. The manager did not wish to be hard on his players, so when he found them with a glass of beer he'd say, "Oh, that's all right, but don't drink too much." Every week they drank a little more, and in the end it smashed the machine.

Alcohol and the worker.—If beer and wine are bad for athletes they are no less bad for workmen, and for the one eternal reason: "Wine is a mocker." The workman who drinks beer thinks he is capable of doing more work, but in fact he does less. Many tests of the effect of the use of small quantities of beer and wine on the keenness of sight, accuracy of marksmanship, endurance, and speed have finally established the fact that alcohol is invariably a handicap to physical efficiency.

MODERATE DRINK AND HEALTH

What science has discovered.—Did our young woman prevent an attack of the "flu" by taking a "stimulant"? Is rock-and-rye good for a bad cold? Is whisky the "milk of the aged" and beer "good for nursing mothers"? Professor Metchnikoff, of the Pasteur Institute, Paris, discovered that the white corpuscles of the blood have the power of destroying disease germs or other foreign matter. They attack the germs by throwing out processes of their protoplasm, inclosing them and afterward digesting them.

The work of the phagocytes.—If microbes or chemical irritants are present in one particular part of the body, these white blood cells leave the blood vessels in the neighborhood in large numbers and stream toward the point affected. They then attack the germs and seek to destroy them. In so doing they are, many of them, in their turn destroyed, and their dead bodies, along with the fluids of the inflamed tissues, form pus, as exhibited in cut or wound, in boil or abscess. Their method of surrounding or swallowing disease germs and waste matter has caused them to be called phagocytes, or cells that devour.

Lowering resistance.—If we remember the toxic action of alcohol upon cell life, it is easy to realize its effect in lowering resistance to disease by narcotizing the phagocytes, the superior white corpuscles, practically "making the policemen drunk." Here, as often, it prepares the way for evils worse than itself and not infrequently more fatal.

The opsonins and their work.—The phagocytes are assisted in cleaning the disease germs out of the body by substances that are poisonous to the microbes. These substances are called opsonins and they grow less in bad health. Dr. Charles E. Stewart, of Battle Creek, Michigan, conducted experiments a few years ago to determine the effect of alcohol upon the "opsonic index," or measure of the bodily resistance to disease. He found the index number indicating normal resistance to the bacillus tuberculosis to be 1.17 and for streptococci 1.12. The average of these same cases after the administration of two ounces of port wine was .73 and .655 respectively, showing a drop in the opsonic power of 37 per cent in the former and 42 per cent in the latter case.

An argument refuted.—Since prohibition came, it has not been uncommon for opponents of the policy to manifest great indignation because "the health of the country was being menaced by the inability of physicians to prescribe alcohol freely." We shall avoid confusion if we call to mind that whisky and brandy have been banished from the United States pharmacopœia; that the United States Public Health Service has branded alcohol as the ally of pneumonia and other diseases; that municipal and State health departments, medical associations, and individual physicians the country over are appealing for abstinence and prohibition. Dr. W. A. Evans, medical editor of the *Chicago Tribune* and former health officer of Chicago, says: "No health authority anywhere advocates the use of alcohol as a medicine, food, or beverage."

What the health boards say.—The antialcohol campaign has at times been pressed with the utmost vigor by the New York City Board of Health and also by health boards in Chicago, Toronto, Indiana, Vermont, and other progressive States and cities. The New York board in a recently published booklet says: "Don't muddle your brain by drinking beer, whisky, or other alcoholic drinks. They always harm you." The Chicago Board of Health, in its war on drink, recently issued a bulletin that says:

The fellow with alcohol in his system is not a good witness as to its effects upon himself, for his mind as well as his body is bribed by the drug and is as full of prejudice as his breath is full of fumes. . . .

Daily moderate drinkers are constantly under the harmful influence of alcohol, since the effects of one drink, as is clearly shown by repeated experiments, do not wear off before the next one is taken.

Our Questions Answered

Alcohol does not increase mental or physical power. It is injurious to athletes and workmen. It breaks the bodily resistance to disease. Its use in medical practice is rapidly being restricted by physicians of high standing to external use. It is opposed by medical associations, the Life Extension Institute, and a long list of the leading hygienists and physicians of the world. Beer is not a healthful summer drink but is, on the contrary, a frequent cause of sunstroke. Alcohol does not warm the body in winter, although it does create a feeling of warmth. This drug does not relieve fatigue or strengthen the weak. It is very injurious to infants and to the elderly; but it succeeds in a truly remarkable way in camouflaging its own effects.

Questions for Discussion

What are some of the common misconceptions as to the beneficial effects of drinking alcohol?

Indicate the dangers of the use of alcohol as a medicine otherwise than by prescription of a physician?

Have you ever known any individual to be changed by alcohol from a highly civilized man to a primitive creature?

What effect has the spread of athletics had upon the consumption of alcohol?

Having in mind persons you know, which are the more prosperous—those who are "moderate" drinkers or those who are abstainers?

What is the result of drinking alcohol upon the power to resist disease?

Do you think that woman is under an even greater obligation than man to abstain from alcohol? If so, why?

With so many opportunities for productive work, do

you think any one earns a living by pandering to the baser appetites of man?

Was the abolition of the saloon an injustice to the saloon keeper himself?

How do you think that physicians ought to be provided with ample alcohol supplies, yet the dangers of abusing their privileges avoided?

But take heed lest by any means this liberty of yours become a stumblingblock to the weak. For if a man see thee who hast knowledge sitting at meat in an idol's temple, will not his conscience, if he is weak, be emboldened to eat things sacrificed to idols? For through thy knowledge he that is weak perisheth, the brother for whose sake Christ died. And thus, sinning against the brethren, and wounding their conscience when it is weak, ye sin against Christ. Wherefore, if meat causeth my brother to stumble, I will eat no flesh for evermore, that I cause not my brother to stumble. (1 Cor. 8. 9-13.)

Jesus made answer and said, A certain man was going down from Jerusalem to Jericho; and he fell among robbers, who both stripped him and beat him, and departed, leaving him half dead. And by chance a certain priest was going down that way: and when he saw him he passed by on the other side. And in like manner a Levite also, when he came to the place, and saw him, passed by on the other side. But a certain Samaritan, as he journeyed, came where he was: and when he saw him, he was moved with compassion, and came to him, and bound up his wounds, pouring on *them* oil and wine; and he set him on his own beast, and brought him to an inn, and took care of him. And on the morrow he took out two shillings, and gave them to the host, and said, Take care of him; and whatsoever thou spendest more, I, when I come back again, will repay thee. (Luke 10. 30-35.)

CHAPTER V

THE PRICE OF CIVILIZATION

The alcohol question presents itself at every corner to every man and woman desirous of solving the great social problems that await solution.

It is a kind of root problem, the settlement of which would necessarily involve an adjustment of innumerable other things which have a destructive effect on every hand. As a mere matter of economy and time this is a question worthy most serious consideration.—*Sir Vesey Strong, Lord Mayor of London.*

THE benefits of a complex social organization impose certain obligations upon every individual. It is well to consider the effect of drink and the drink traffic upon ourselves as individuals, but it is much more important to consider the effect of the drink traffic upon our community and our country. The *American Brewers' Review,* in March, 1914, said editorially:

With the increase of population, the gathering of the people closer together in cities, the greater division of labor and specialization of effort, have come a closer dependence of man upon man, a more constant, intimate, and vital contact, and, hence, a greater restriction in the freedom of individual movement. We submit to-day to restrictions which, a hundred years ago, would have been considered monstrous. Regulations for the public safety, the general health, the facilitating of traffic and industry, minute prescriptions for the conduct of elections, are established and acquiesced in from the conviction that without them there would be chaos.

And at another time it admitted:

The so-called personal-liberty argument in behalf of alcoholic drink loses more and more of its force. Consideration of the public welfare continues to grow and overshadow the rights of the individual. The drink question must be fought out upon the ultimate foundation of morals, hygiene, and social order—in other words, the public welfare. If the public welfare requires the suppression of the alcoholic drink traffic, it should be suppressed.

Drink, Long Life, and Worth-While Living

Alcohol and the death rate.—City boards of health are justified in their propaganda against alcohol. Says Warner:

Health, physical and mental, is first among the essentials of personal well-being and happiness. Sickness imposes upon the country a vast economic loss each year. The efficiency of the people is reduced, and valuable lives are wasted by preventable illness. By its effect upon the body, its power to weaken resistance to disease, and by its effect upon the standard of living, alcohol contributes directly and indirectly to a swollen death rate. The crude death rate as reported by the Bureau of the Census for 1917 was 14.3; for 1918 it was 18.1, but this was an influenza year and therefore it is hardly available for purposes of comparison. In 1921, after one full year of prohibition, the death rate had fallen to 11.6.

One business that suffered.—The writer at one time was sitting in a hotel lobby at Massillon, Ohio, waiting to address a Methodist Conference that evening. A commercial traveler sat down by him and was asked:

"Well, how's business?"

"Pretty poor," he replied.

"I am sorry to hear that," the writer said.

"You wouldn't be sorry if you knew what I sell," the drummer answered. "I sell coffins."

A declining death rate.—He went on to explain that during the two years previous to the conversation, which was after the coming of prohibition, the death rate had greatly declined. There had been a falling off in the demand for coffins, especially, he said, in the demand for coffins for children. All over the United States there was noted a sudden decrease in the death rate—so sudden that it was very distinct from the normal gradual decline due to improvement in the practice of medicine and better sanitation. This sudden decline was most noticeable in cities that were formerly large consumers of beer and whisky. It would hardly be an excessive estimate to say that prohibition has been the direct cause of saving thousands of lives annually. Bunnell Phelps, an authority on mortality statistics, disbelieving the oft-heard statement of prohibitionists that the saloon killed a hundred thousand people annually, conducted an investigation some years before prohibition and came to the conclusion that alcohol was responsible, directly and indirectly, for sixty-six thousand deaths in the United States yearly. This figure means that one man died every eight minutes due to the traffic in alcohol, and that our licensed saloons murdered each year more Americans than were killed on the battlefield during the World War.

The experience of insurance companies.—The New York Life Insurance Company, in a scholarly study reporting the experience of various insurance companies, found alcohol consumption to be a formidable enemy to life. The Northwestern Life found the chances of death to daily users of beer was, compared with that of total abstainers, as 133 is to 100. The Metropolitan Life Insurance Company, in a recent report, states the average death rate for each 1,000 of population was 14.2 for the first four years before national prohibition and 12.2 for the four years following national prohibition. According to their experience the death rate from alcoholism for each 100,000 industrial policyholders was 4 in 1917, a year before the war restrictions on drink, and 2.8 in 1924. Deaths from alcoholism are seldom correctly reported, as there is a certain stigma attached to such an end, so that both figures probably should be larger; but the comparison would hold true.

Hospital statistics.—City statistics and statistics of hospitals are similar. Dr. George O'Hanlon, sixteen years general medical superintendent of Bellevue and Allied Hospitals in New York, says that in 1924 they handled only about 4,000 alcoholic cases, whereas before the Volstead Act they handled from 10,000 to 12,000 a year. The figures showing deaths from cirrhosis of the liver, which is a drink disease, would teach the same lesson. The death rate from these drink diseases has increased since the first prohibition year, although it seems that we are working back toward the satisfactory figures of 1920. At no time under prohibition, however, has the record been worse than it was under license.

Deaths in a great city.—The death rate in New York City from tuberculosis has been almost cut in half. Many other things contributed to this reduction in the case of tuberculosis, but prohibition undoubtedly was a factor.

The Christian attitude.—Now, what is the law of the kingdom of love in view of these facts? Life is precious to the Creator. Suppose two men are at a dinner at which drinks are being served. One man quietly declines; the other drinks and says, "Prohibition is all right for the workingman or for the man who cannot control his appetite, but I drink or leave it alone and I don't propose to pay any attention to a law that interferes with my private concerns." On the same evening a workman buys a cheap synthetic whisky from a bootlegger, kills his wife in a frenzied rage, and commits suicide. Is there not a connection between the two incidents? Which man at the dinner was true to the obligation of Christian brotherhood? To which man would Christ have said, "Well done"?

ALCOHOL AND INSANITY

Decrease in alcoholic insanity.—Alcoholic cases constituted only 3.7 per cent of the total admissions to hospitals for the insane in the United States in 1922 as against 10.1 per cent in 1910, according to new statistics of the United States Census Bureau.

The change has been brought about [say proof sheets of the forthcoming Census Bureau Report on Patients in Hospitals for Mental Diseases] by a change in the habits of the people with respect to drinking and by the eighteenth amendment and laws prohibiting the manufacture and sale of alcoholic beverages. As these laws now apply to the whole country, a reduction in the percentage of alcoholic cases is noted in nearly every State in 1922; but the marked differences in the percentages in the several States in 1922 indicate very unequal observance of such laws.

Sobriety and sanity.—It is clear that sobriety increases a man's chance of keeping out of the insane hospital, and also that society, if it will, can protect itself against part of the misery and the expense of insanity by promoting observance and enforcement of the prohibition laws. As the Census Bureau statistics are for 1922, it may be asked, What is the trend of alcoholic cases since 1922? There are of course no complete national statistics. But the Scientific Temperance Federation, of Boston, has obtained data for 13 consecutive years—1912–24—from 42 State hospitals for the insane in 9 States. These combined hospital records in 1922 showed practically the same percentage of alcoholic cases in first admissions. In 1924 their percentage of first alcoholic cases (4.9) had risen slightly above that of 1922, but it was still almost a third lower than in any of the normal preprohibition years of the period 1912–17. It was nearly 50 per cent lower than in 1917, when an apparently upward trend was interrupted by the influence of war sobriety and war restrictions on the liquor traffic. A very low point was reached in the first prohibition year (2.2). Such increase as has since taken place occurred chiefly in 1921 and 1922, with a distant slackening in the rate of increase in 1923 and 1924.

DRINK AND CRIME

The effect of prohibition upon crime.—America must plead guilty to being the most murderous nation on earth. And our people who are concerned by this fact are quite excusable for being confused as to the effect of prohibition upon crime. What are the facts? In the first place it is an undoubted fact that the licensed drink trade caused crime. The Committee of Fifty, a distinguished body that investigated the drink question many years ago, found that approximately 50 per cent of crime was due to the consumption of alcoholic liquor. Nearly every judge of distinction before prohibition asserted that drink filled our penal institutions. A report of the manager of the Allegheny County (Pennsylvania) Work House declared that of 3,798 persons received 3,472 were alcohol addicts. There can also be no doubt that prohibition States, on the whole, had a more favorable crime rate than the license States. The effect of the suppression of drink upon crime was never more strikingly illustrated than just after the San Francisco earthquake. During the time of demoralization following that disaster the saloons were closed, and, on May 5, the *Daily Chronicle* said that San Francisco "was a city without crime."

Causes of crime increase.—Crime statistics are very confusing. In America the various States and municipalities keep them so loosely and in such varied manner that we can arrive at truth only by very careful study. The general impression is that crime has greatly increased under prohibition. An investigation covering 300 cities, made by the World League Against Alcoholism, shows a total number of arrests from 1913 to 1916 of 1,756,078. For the first four years of prohibition the total was 2,040,700—a considerable increase. Wet propaganda would present these bare facts as an indictment of prohibition; but upon further examination we find that the population of these cities had increased from 29,800,000 to 34,600,000. Furthermore, automobiles had vastly increased in number, partly because of prohibition prosperity; and traffic violations were included in the total number of arrests given for the prohibition years. What this means is illustrated by the fact that traffic violations in New York City alone increased from 11,276 in 1915 to 141,110 in 1924. This throws a very different light on the figures, does it not?

Arrests for drunkenness.—Now consider the arrests for drunkenness. In these 300 cities in 1920 arrests for drunkenness were 8.7 for each 1,000 population; whereas in 1916, just previous to the war restrictions on the sale of liquor, they had been 24.1 for each 1,000 population. There is further information to be had. The second prohibition year showed an increase under the influence of wet propaganda and bootleg enterprise to 11.3, the third prohibition year a further increase to 15.3, the fourth prohibition year to 17.4; but the fifth prohibition year showed a decline to 13.4. The nation is having the same experience as prohibition States, and eventually we shall once again reach the low mark of 1920 as the force of propaganda inciting to violation of the law passes.

Increase in spectacular crime.—We must be very honest about this. There is no doubt that banditry, hold-ups, and similar spectacular crimes committed by those verging upon maturity have increased. It is the reports of these crimes that occupy so much newspaper space and create the impression that all crime has increased. Also, arrests made in enforcement of the prohibition law add largely to the total; but they are worthless for purposes of com-

parison unless on the other side we include violations of
the license law, which were very common before prohibition.

Decrease in juvenile delinquency.—Note this in passing
—that juvenile delinquency, contrary to the general impression, has sharply decreased. It will be said that prohibition is not responsible for all these good results; that
other factors enter into the case. Certainly. Just how
much do you think prohibition has contributed to the improvement, and just how far do you think prohibition is
responsible where there has been lack of improvement?
Young men and young women are more violent. If liquors
figure in this situation, should we blame it on prohibition
or on the antiprohibitionists who tell them that prohibition
is a farce and an outrage, and that the law should be
flouted? To what extent is the war to be blamed? Is
the availability to criminals of automobiles a cause of
crime? To what extent do chaotic social and religious conditions demoralize young people? How about the failure
to Americanize the "second generation" of the "new immigration"? Most of our bandit youths of to-day come from
this group.

Decrease in number of prisoners.—The Bureau of the
Census recently completed an enumeration of prisoners in
the penal institutions of the United States as of July 1,
1917, and July 1, 1922. This showed an increase of 7.1
per cent in the number of prisoners confined on July 1,
1922; but there were only 282 institutions not reporting
on July 1, 1922, as compared with 1,076 not reporting
July 1, 1917. The ratio to 100,000 of population in 1922
was only 137.4 as compared with 137.2 in 1917, and we are
therefore justified in believing that, taking into consideration the larger number of institutions reporting in 1922,
there was an actual decrease in the number of prisoners
for each 100,000 of population. A study of the bulletin
reveals: (1) There was a sharp decrease in the number
of prisoners in States that formerly had licensed saloons.
(2) There was an increase in the number of prisoners in
those States which were under prohibition prior to 1917.
Those States had already reaped the benefit of their prohibition policy and suffered from the natural crime-in-
creasing tendency of the war period. Hastings H. Hart,

President of the American Prison Association in 1921–22, in commenting upon the bulletin says: "If it had not been for prohibition these twenty-eight States (which were wet before 1917) like the twenty prohibition States would doubtless have shown a very large increase in consequence of the war."

DRINK IN RELATION TO POVERTY AND DISTRESS

Poverty and pauperism.—"Ye have the poor always with you," said our Master. There is a difference between poverty and pauperism. Poverty is respectable; pauperism is either shameful or one of the greatest of all misfortunes. The number of paupers enumerated in almshouses increased at each enumeration from 1880 to 1910 but decreased from 1910 to 1923. The number for each hundred thousand of population in 1910 was 96; in 1923 it had reached the remarkably low figure of 58.4.

Mr. Horace G. Wadlin, one-time chief of the Bureau of Statistics of Labor of Massachusetts, in a report on the relation of the liquor traffic to pauperism, crime and insanity, written some years ago, said:

Out of thirty-two hundred and thirty paupers—this being the total number found in the institutions during twelve consecutive months—twenty-one hundred and eight, or about sixty-five in every hundred (65.26 per cent) were addicted to the use of liquor. The excessive drinkers numbered five hundred and five, or about sixteen in every one hundred (15.63 per cent) of all the paupers. The total abstainers numbered eight hundred and sixty-six, or about twenty-seven in every one hundred (26.81 per cent) of all the paupers. Of the total abstainers, however, four hundred and twenty-nine were minors, two hundred and eighty-one being under ten years of age. There were also thirty-one minors addicted to the use of liquor. Excluding all the minors, whether total abstainers or not, we have twenty-seven hundred and fifty-two paupers of adult years, of whom two thousand and seventy-seven, or about seventy-five in every one hundred (75.47 per cent), were addicted to the use of liquor, including five hundred and four excessive drinkers and fifteen hundred and seventy-three drinkers not classed excessive.

Of the whole number of paupers, 47.74 per cent, or nearly forty-eight in every one hundred, had one or both parents intemperate.

Of the whole number 39.44 per cent, or about thirty-nine in every one hundred, attributed their pauperism to their own intemperate habits; about five in every one hundred considered their pauperism due to the intemperance of their parents, one or both; and several in every one hundred attributed their pauperism to the intemperance of those upon whom they were dependent, other than parents.

Decrease in destitution.—In Chicago, in Boston, in New York City, and in a score of other cities there was reported a sudden decrease in destitution after prohibition. The United Charities of Chicago said in 1921: "There is a decrease of 20 per cent in the number of families whose difficulties are combined with illegitimacy, begging, and nonsupport during the last two years. The latter factor is fast disappearing. During the same two years social diseases among these families had diminished 22 per cent." An investigation made by the Family Welfare Society of Boston revealed that prohibition resulted in a 74-per-cent decrease in drink cases coming to charitable organizations in 1922 as compared with the year 1917. The investigation covered twenty-one cities.

What the Salvation Army finds.—No one in America knows more about the poor than the beloved commander of the Salvation Army—Evangeline Booth. Out of the wealth of her personal experience and the reports of her organization she has drawn the following statement:

Our social secretaries tell us that drunkenness among the men frequenting our hotels and industrial homes has almost entirely disappeared. In one of our hotels there are 120 men, with banking accounts of considerable amounts, who previously could not keep a dollar for twenty-four hours.

Our officers engaged in prison work report that the penal institutions are rapidly being depopulated. Many of them, like Paterson, New Jersey (reduced from 150 to 14), and Hackensack, in the same State, are converting their jails into dwelling apartments. Prisons in other places are being turned into schools.

Needless to say, the experience of our own slum officers emphasizes the benefits. "Father buys us clothes since prohibition. He used to drink all the money up," said a little girl in Hell's Kitchen last week. They find the home better cared for and less divided; and where they used to get mother and children only to the meeting, the whole family now attends.

The entire Army world seems to have heard of our boozers' day—how year by year we have celebrated the Thanksgiving holiday from six in the morning, collecting the drunks from the park benches, feeding them and sobering them up and saving them with huge and lasting results. But last year they were not there, and so we gave the day to the poorest children of the great city.

In large numbers we gathered the underprivileged boys —the little lads who sell the newspapers, the waifs and strays, and even the crippled who eke out their unhappy existence in the unchanged miseries of the slums. Never shall I forget the upturned faces of the five thousand of New York's poorest under fourteen as they lifted their childish voices in the song which must still echo somewhere in heaven: "Yes, Jesus loves me: the Bible tells me so."

And this seems to me to be one of the most significant of the early results of prohibition. It means that in the future we shall have less to do with the grave and more to do with the cradle; less binding up of life's broken plants and more training of life's untrammeled vines; that more of our energy, our ingenious methods, will be thrown into work of prevention, which in the final analysis must be so much more valuable to the home, the nation, and the kingdom of God than even the most worthy work of cure.

A FAIR QUESTION

In the light of these facts is it, in your opinion, a matter of any importance whatever that some people may be put to slight inconvenience because saloons are not open on every corner to supply alcoholic drinks to satisfy their perverted appetites? The drinking of wine or beer may not be a sin in itself, but can we call it less in view of what the evil means to such a large number of our people?

QUESTIONS FOR DISCUSSION

A man on a desert island, far from civilization, becomes drunk. Another man in Chicago, charged with industrial responsibility, takes a drink. How does the moral quality of these acts differ. Which is the greater misstep?

How many things have contributed to the decline of the death rate in the United States since prohibition? How many of these favorable conditions were themselves, in part at least, the product of prohibition?

What evidence can you cite that crime is increasing? What kind of crime? How do you meet the person who blames prohibition with the increased number of arrests? Is it fair to include traffic arrests and similar violations in the comparison between crime conditions in prohibition years and in wet years?

A young man whose parents wasted their money in drink when there was a saloon on every corner now has ample funds to attend school and drive an automobile. Coming from a family with no social or religious standards, he is so excited by his prosperity that he is guilty of spectacular misbehavior and finally of crime. Where is the logic lame that says that this crime was caused by prohibition? Name other things than prohibition that by the same logic could be declared inadvisable?

To what extent do you know of families that have been relieved from poverty by the passing of the saloon? In what ways are they worth more to society than they were?

And I saw a new heaven and a new earth: for the first heaven and the first earth are passed away; and the sea is no more. And I saw the holy city, new Jerusalem, coming down out of heaven from God, made ready as a bride adorned for her husband. And I heard a great voice out of the throne saying, Behold, the tabernacle of God is with men, and he shall dwell with them, and they shall be his peoples, and God himself shall be with them, *and be* their God: and he shall wipe away every tear from their eyes; and death shall be no more; neither shall there be mourning, nor crying, nor pain any more: the first things are passed away. And he that sitteth on the throne said, Behold, I make all things new. And he saith, Write: for these words are faithful and true. And he said unto me, They are come to pass. I am the Alpha and the Omega, the beginning and the end. I will give unto him that is athirst of the fountain of the water of life freely. He that overcometh shall inherit these things; and I will be his God, and he shall be my son. But for the fearful, and unbelieving, and abominable, and murderers, and fornicators, and sorcerers, and idolaters, and all liars, their part *shall be* in the lake that burneth with fire and brimstone; which is the second death. (Rev. 21. 1-8.)

CHAPTER VI

NEW PROBLEMS IN A NEW WORLD

I have stated repeatedly my conviction that a person who has attained to adult age and who requires alcohol as a food or stimulant or who has acquired the alcohol habit may attain to a certain degree of richness in mind, body, or estate; but so far as the evolution or stability of the race is concerned, it would be far better for the world had he or she never been born into it.—*Theodore Bulkley Hyslop, M.D.*

THE modern highly organized state of society affects every aspect of human relations. For instance, it is idle for our great cities to claim a right to home rule on the liquor problem now that they have acquired such a large proportion of the population and such a preponderant financial and social power. The father and mother who live in a small Illinois town, from which they have driven the drink menace, cannot be expected to be indifferent to the state of affairs in Chicago when they know that it is nearly inevitable that their sons and daughters will seek in Chicago larger business opportunities and more significant social recognition. For generations there has been a shift to the cities. Before prohibition most of our cities were saloon controlled; to-day the cities of Chicago, New York, and Baltimore complain bitterly that they are unfairly deprived of their due influence in State legislation and administration. The bald truth is that the people of those several States feel that those great cities, because of the un-Americanized part of their population and their organized corrupt vote, would administer the affairs of Illinois, New York, and Maryland in the interest of the drink trade and other corrupt specialized interests if they were allowed to dominate the State Legislatures and the executive departments. Improvements in methods of transportation, which have made the American people almost a seasonally migrating population, have given every American an intimate personal interest in the society of

every part of America and particularly in every part of his
own State.

The Liquor Evil and the City

The burden of the cities.—The interest of the country
in the city drink question is very practical. At one time
in Nebraska the three urban counties of Hall, Douglas,
and Lancaster, containing one half of all the saloons in the
State, furnished 236 inmates for each 100,000 population
to the State institutions, while the remainder of the State
furnished only 99 for each 100,000 of population. According to the census of 1910 the city districts of the United
States furnished four times as many alcoholic insane to the
nation's asylums as did the rural districts. The country
folks of America were paying taxes in 1910 to support the
alcoholic insane created by city toleration of saloons. It
would hardly be unsafe to say that very few, if any, uplift
movements in any State have been consistently favored by
the cities of the State.

The growing influence of the city.—Just as improved
transportation facilities bring to the city the produce from
the country, so in turn the wider circulation of city newspapers, the invention of the radio, and the presence on
every country piano of New York music, on every small-
town stage of New York performances, are carrying the
leadership of the city into village and rural communities.
Slang coined by New York cartoonists and vaudeville ar-
tists is common on the lips of farm hands in Wyoming and
Arkansas. New York girls paint their lips, and in due
time the girls of Turkey Bend do the same thing. New
York skirts rise knee high, and so do the skirts of Clover
Bottom. Paris dictates that hats shall be larger, and in a
few weeks the fact is known on remote farms. The boys
in the sawmill towns of the Pacific Coast or in the trading
villages of the far South wear thirty-inch trousers because
the boys of Columbia University wear them—or are supposed to wear them. The influence of the city has been
extended to the country to a degree which indicates that
the country must either accept the city standard of morals
or impose upon the city legislation that will protect the
historic moral standards of America.

THE AGE OF MACHINERY

The automobile and the liquor evil.—"Booze had to go out when modern industry and the motor car came in. Upon only one condition can the nation safely let it come back—that is, if we are willing to abolish modern industry and the motor car," said Henry Ford, the man who has done more than any other to make the automobile available to the American of moderate means. It is hard for Americans to realize how much more important is the place of machinery in American life than it is in the life of any other people. It is responsible, perhaps, for our "materialism," but it is also responsible for our prosperity and our comfort. The advocates of the return of the drink traffic surely fail to realize that what they are asking is absolutely impossible in view of the readjustments that have already been made in our national life under prohibition. Consider the automobile. It appears on our streets to-day not only in the charge of mature and responsible people, but driven by the immature, the reckless, and, what is more important, the unintelligent and the unstable. It is quite safe to say that thousands of cars upon our city streets are being driven at this very time by feeble-minded people or people whose mental power is little greater than that of the feeble-minded. The fact that a new automobile can be bought for a few hundred dollars, and that a second-hand automobile can be bought for fifty dollars or a little more has made available to every grade of intelligence and character an instrument of inspiring power. We are troubled by drunken drivers, but what is our hazard from those "driving while drunk" to-day compared with what it would be if a saloon were open on every corner, or if liquor were readily available at any other place of sale? It is said that many automobile accidents are caused by simple fatigue, by food poisoning, which slightly blurs the vision or slows the muscular reactions. What a menace, then, is even one drink of liquor, even one pint of beer, when it is taken by a man responsible for driving an automobile! His vision, as has been proved by scientific experiments, is poorer, while his sense of confidence is vastly greater. The reactions of his muscles to the orders of his brain are very much slower, but "wine the mocker" makes him think that they are quicker. The liquor traffic in any recognized and legal form would make every city street in America a place of horror and death.

The significance of machinery in industry.—The American theory of the maximum use of machinery, of quantity production, and of well-paid efficiency is conquering the industrial world. That theory cannot stand up without the safety-first aid of the prohibition law. On October 6, 1914, the National Safety Council, whose members employed more than a million men, adopted a unanimous resolution in favor of business prohibition and total abstinence. The shops of the Bessemer and Lake Erie Railroad, a subsidiary of the United States Steel Corporation, at one time inserted in the pay envelopes of their employees a slip bearing the pictures of a keg of beer and a sack of flour with the query "Which do you buy?" This concern also organized a water-wagon club and succeeded in enrolling thousands of its employees. A typical poster was as follows:

THE LAST MAN
HIRED;
THE FIRST MAN
FIRED;
THE MAN WHO
DRINKS!

In the office of the Board of Temperance, Prohibition, and Public Morals of the Methodist Episcopal Church is a poster, mutilated by tacks and covered with machine grease, taken from a wall of the Gier Pressed Steel Company, Lansing, Michigan. It reads:

YOU CAN'T DRINK AND MAKE GOOD

MODERN BUSINESS SETS PACE TOO FAST FOR DRINKING MAN'S MIND TO KEEP UP—HE IS NOT IN THE RUNNING

Science Proves by Delicate Instruments of Precision That He Thinks, Sees, Hears, and Acts More Slowly Than the Man Who doesn't Drink.

A dollar watch will stand a great deal more sand than a hundred-dollar one. That will explain why some men can drink quantities of liquor and brag that it doesn't injure them—and it will explain why a few drinks are so injurious to another.

Bright business ideas, ambition, energy, and execution fade under the influence of alcohol like a dream to be replaced by air castles, "large talk," laziness, sluggishness, and neglect.

These conditions are not only found in the drunkard who drinks all the liquor he can get but are even more strongly marked in the steady, three-or-four-drinks-a-day drunkard.

Slow poisoning—quick poisoning—and physicians have always reckoned slow poisoning the surest.

If these things were true before prohibition and if they brought the industrial forces inside of the prohibition movement, how much more true are they to-day, when the place of well-managed machinery in our economic prosperity has become much greater!

The Immigration Problem

The new immigration.—But there are even more delicate problems involved in the consideration of drink as a social factor. We have introduced into our society millions upon millions of immigrants who have mainly gone to our cities. This recent immigration is of a new character. We are not disposed to say that it is inferior to the old immigration. The peoples now arriving are not inferior; they are simply met with difficulties that, by hindering the grafting of their excellencies upon the fundamental character contributed by the makers of the nation, imposes upon us a new obligation. We need their art, we need their music, we need their sense of beauty, we need their generous impulses; but, above all, we need to establish these characteristics as branches upon the sturdy trunk of Americanism. But we did not need these people as saloon keepers (in many parts of the country they constituted the majority of our saloon keepers) ; nor did we need them as opponents of the American policy of prohibition.

Bootlegging among foreign-born people.—The greatest hindrance to the absorption and amalgamation of the new immigration was the saloon and the liquor traffic, and the greatest hindrance to-day is still the liquor traffic. For it is probable that much more than half of all the bootleg liquor consumed in the East to-day is consumed by foreign-born people, and it has been established by authoritative

statement that from three fourths to nine tenths of all the
liquor bootlegged is sold by foreign-born people. The
cutting off of much of the flow of immigration gives us a
more possible task as well as a new opportunity to make
these newcomers real American citizens. No greater con-
tribution could be made to the Americanization of the
foreigners in the country than the complete elimination of
drink as a social factor.

PROHIBITION AND THE NEGRO

Bootlegging among Negroes. — Under slavery the
Negroes were protected from alcohol. Consequently, they
developed no high degree of ability to resist its evil effects.
It is well known that if a disease becomes prevalent in a
community where it has not existed for some generations
past it is peculiarly virulent. This is true of alcoholism,
as is commonly observed in regard to the Indians. At the
present time the Negroes, particularly in the Northern
States, where they have flocked by the hundreds of thousands as industrial laborers, are subject to energetic ex-
ploitation by the illicit liquor trade. They consume considerable quantities of bootleg liquor because of their
general ignorance as to its true character. More important is the fact that they are used as retail bootleggers
by white men who produce moonshine liquor. Negroes
often protest in the public prints against the supine
abandoning of their residential sections to violators of the
prohibition law.

How prohibition has helped the Negro race.—It is hard,
however, to overestimate the value of prohibition to the
colored man. During the saloon days the Negro was a
particularly pitiful victim of the grogshop, which frequently
not only ruined his health and broke up his home but
turned him into a violent brute and brought him not
seldom to an equally brutish end. Even after most of the
Southern States went dry, Negroes in the South were exploited by the liquor wholesalers of Cincinnati, Louisville,
Jacksonville, and other cities. Illustrated circulars fairly
flooded the cabins of the corn and cotton hands, and politicians who desired to make use of the Negro vote (which
in some parts of the South was considerable and in other

parts practically did not exist) frequently had their political documents printed on the back of liquor circulars and called attention to the fact that certain wholesalers were deserving of patronage. Booker T. Washington, in 1914, in a letter to the Board of Temperance declared:

When all the facts are considered, strong drink, I believe, is one of the chief causes of Negro crime in the South. In prohibition Macon County, Alabama, where I live, there are about twenty-two thousand Negroes and four thousand whites. The sheriff of my county recently reported that he had only one deputy and did not have enough work to keep him busy.

Dr. Harvey W. Wiley, writing in *Good Housekeeping*, gives the following picturesque description of a prohibition town in the "black belt":

Recently, in one of the interior counties in Arkansas, I was shown about the county seat by one of the big business men of the community. It was Saturday afternoon. Hundreds of vehicles of all sorts, drawn by mules, most of which were in good condition, were picketed around the public square. The great department store, which my guide owned, was filled with colored people. They were buying most liberally and were extremely well dressed and well behaved. I was struck with their appearance and prosperity and happiness. I was curious to know why it was that these people seemed so much better off than those I had seen in other localities. I asked the proprietor, who was freely giving credit to his customers, if he did not lose on many accounts. He replied, "Never one." "How do you account for their prosperity?" I asked. "Strictly enforced prohibition," was his answer. "If we were to permit the saloon to come into this county again, it would wreck all our prosperity; it would ruin my business and send this town back fifty years."

We do not need, therefore, to go to big business for our examples; we can draw them from the interior counties of Arkansas, where big business is little known. It is the same old story everywhere. It is the old irreconcilable fight between alcohol and efficiency. Between the two there can be no compromise. That nation is best prepared to endure . . . when temperance in all things prevails, when abstinence from all harmful drugs is practiced, when alcohol in any form as a beverage is unknown.

BOOTLEGGING DOOMED

While the elements of our population opposed by tradition, training, and habit to prohibition must be reckoned with, there can be no question that bootlegging is doomed.   As a federal judge recently stated in his charge to a jury:

> The hope in the hearts of a minority of this country that liquor is coming back is fast dying out. The bootlegger and the blockader are fighting a hopeless cause.   The United States has never been whipped in any war yet and it will not be whipped in the battle which has been joined by these enemies of American homes, of American traditions, of American institutions and of American destiny. The only war, I pray God, that this republic will ever be forced to engage in hereafter is the war to drive liquor eternally out of existence in our land. . . .
>
> This court believes in the enforcement of the laws which have been enacted to govern the sale and use of whisky. I am no fanatic on the subject but I do have the conviction that ninety per cent of the crimes that have been committed in this nation, ninety per cent of the suicides, the heartbreaks, the wrecked homes, and the destroyed wealth, property and life of this republic, is distinctly traceable to the whisky traffic. I am supported in this opinion by all the intelligent sentiment of the times.

QUESTIONS FOR DISCUSSION

On what grounds have the country districts a right to "coerce" the cities in an effort to suppress the liquor traffic? How is the influence of the nearest city felt in your rural districts?   How is the country resident himself in a sense a citizen of the nearest metropolitan district?

How has the automobile increased crime and misbehavior in your community? To what extent is drinking a factor in this? What are your reasons for thinking there would be more drink-caused crime in connection with the use of automobiles if the legalized liquor traffic should return?

A young man takes two drinks of whisky or a pint of beer, enters his automobile, and is involved in an accident. Apparently he was not drunk. Do you think the drink he had taken had anything to do with the accident? On what medical or scientific ground? Should he be punished for driving while intoxicated?

How many of the foreign-born or children of foreign-born people in your community have ever heard any reasons for the passage of the prohibition law? What can the church do to inform them? Are the bootleggers in your community foreign-born? If so, are they managed by native-born Americans?

How does alcohol consumption where you live affect order and good feeling between colored people and white people?

And he said unto his disciples, It is impossible but that occasions of stumbling should come; but woe unto him through whom they come! It were well for him if a millstone were hanged about his neck, and he were thrown into the sea, rather than that he should cause one of these little ones to stumble. (Luke 17. 1, 2.)

Every one that doeth sin doeth also lawlessness; and sin is lawlessness. And ye know that he was manifested to take away sins; and in him is no sin. Whosoever abideth in him sinneth not: whosoever sinneth hath not seen him, neither knoweth him. *My* little children, let no man lead you astray: he that doeth righteousness is righteous, even as he is righteous: he that doeth sins is of the devil; for the devil sinneth from the beginning. To this end was the Son of God manifested, that he might destroy the works of the devil. Whosoever is begotten of God doeth no sin, because his seed abideth in him: and he cannot sin, because he is begotten of God. In this the children of God are manifest, and the children of the devil: whosoever doeth not righteousness is not of God, neither he that loveth not his brother. For this is the message which ye heard from the beginning, that we should love one another. (1 John 3. 4-11.)

CHAPTER VII

THE ECONOMIC BENEFITS OF PROHIBITION

There can be no doubt of the economic benefits of prohibition. Viewing the temperance question only from this angle, prohibition has proved its case. I think increased temperance over the land is responsible for a good share of the enormously increased efficiency in production, which statistics gathered by the Department of Commerce show to have followed passage of the dry law.—*Herbert Hoover, Secretary of Commerce.*

GILBERT K. CHESTERTON has said that in his opinion the one great argument for prohibition—namely, that it increases efficiency—is the greatest of all arguments against it. Obviously he considered it a scheme of the employer to wring the last bit of labor out of employees and to increase his own profits at the expense of the happiness of the men who work for him. There is no doubt that many large employers were led to favor prohibition because they believed it would increase their own profits. Many of these men, with a most reprehensible lack of sportsmanship, keep their own cellars stocked, although they are banking the profits of the abstinence of their workmen.

WHAT PROHIBITION HAS MEANT TO THE WORKER

Some benefits.—Prohibition, however, has not imposed upon the workingman harder conditions of labor than he had. The sober workingman is the better able to deal with the employer in controversies involving hours of work and scale of pay. With less fatiguing effort he makes more for his employer. In adding to the country's stocks of goods he is adding to the commodities available for his own use. And with his greater efficiency he can insist that he receive as compensation a larger share of the product of his labor.

The workingman's diet.—"Tell me what you eat, and I will tell you what you are," says the doctor. This is especially true of children. Informed physicians say that the diet of children in one generation determines to a great extent the health and strength of the adults of the next generation. Food must be varied, must include cereals; but particularly there must be a sufficiency of green vegetables, fruit, milk, and butter. Ten years ago the table of the workingman was poorly supplied with these essentials. His children lived upon coarse and heavy foods, with little or no milk, and with green vegetables only a few months of the year. The Department of Agriculture of the United States, reports an increase in the consumption of milk from 36,500,000,000 pounds in 1917 to 52,772,000,000 pounds in 1924. The Thatcher Manufacturing Company, largest makers of milk bottles in the country, in the first year of prohibition wrote to the Board of Temperance, Prohibition, and Public Morals of the Methodist Episcopal Church:

The "consumption" of milk bottles in this country increased during the first six months of this year fully thirty-five per cent. In talking with a large number of milk dealers in New York, Philadelphia, Baltimore, Washington, Chicago, Detroit, and other places they have all of them expressed the belief that the increased consumption of milk and, therefore, the increased demand for milk bottles were caused by prohibition. We certainly believe that this is true.

It is probably true that the increase in the use of milk is largely due to the greater consumption of milk by children in families where it was not formerly afforded. However, the workingman himself is using more of this health-giving food, getting it at soda fountains and other public places and consuming it by the pint or quart at his lunch hour, at which time it has replaced the old can of beer. All of us have observed the greater consumption of winter fruits and vegetables produced in Florida, California, and other favored climes. Formerly oranges were seen in a workingman's home only at Christmas. Now the morning orange is almost an American habit. Doctor Saleeby, the great eugenist of England, attributes the robust health of the present American generation to milk and light, which may be paraphrased as a good diet and good housing.

The workingman's home.—Prohibition not only has contributed to the workingman's table: it has given him better clothing and better housing, has helped him to protect his family by insurance, and has placed an automobile in his garage. A report of the Alcoholic Liquor Committee of the House of Representatives states that there has been an increase in the erection of small houses, principally for the workingman, amounting to 300 per cent. "Prohibition has been a boon of inestimable value to building and loan associations," says W. R. Adair, vice-president of the United States League of Building and Loan Associations. The assets of these organizations have doubled. Furniture production increased 41 per cent from 1921 to 1924. There are 18,000,000 automobiles, and in 1924 America spent $4,000,000,000 for cars, repairs, and gasoline, incidentally paying $470,000,000 in taxes; exceeding the revenue from the liquor trade, which, to a considerable extent, the automobile industry has replaced. The average monthly amount of ordinary life insurance written in 1924 was $533,764,-000, while in 1917, the last really wet year, it was only $213,193,000. More significant still is the increase in industrial insurance, usually taken by workingmen, from $61,484,000 monthly, in 1917, to $292,094,000 monthly, in 1924. And (bright promise for the future) the expenditure for public schools increased between 1920 and 1922 by more than 50 per cent.

WHY THE SUPPRESSION OF THE LIQUOR TRADE BENEFITS BUSINESS

Liquor a nonproducer.—The reason that business benefits by prohibition is to be found in the fact that the liquor traffic is not a productive trade. The United States spent before prohibition $2,438,000,000 a year for intoxicating liquors. All this money was lost. The money spent at retail for drink did not return anything of value to the man who spent it. That is a characteristic that the transaction has in common with every other illegitimate transaction. Certainly the money did not go out of circulation, certainly it was respent, in large part, for legitimate commodities; but that does not relieve the transaction of

its stigma. For the same thing is true of the money the
highwayman acquires by his nefarious conduct. The same
thing is true of the money the prostitute acquires by
debasing her body and spreading disease in the community.
The expenditure of this vast sum did not register the
creation or exchange of value. Long ago Adam Smith said:

> All the labor expended in producing strong drink is utterly
> unproductive; it adds nothing to the wealth of the community.
> A wise man works and earns wages and spends his wages so
> that he may work again. Employers, taken all around, do not
> pay more wages to total abstainers, but the latter contribute
> more to their own and fellow workers' wages fund than do
> the drinkers.

Every bit of material used in the manufacture of liquor
was destroyed so far as its value to the world was concerned.
Every dollar of wages paid represented waste of valuable
time that should have contributed to the world's wealth.
Every cent paid for liquor over the bar represented loss.
No trade can be accounted of value to the nation if it
merely produces or supplies consumption. It must also
contribute to the conservation of products and energies,
making its output reproduce all of the material and labor
it represents and add something to the nation's reserve
of wealth.

What this waste would be to-day.—If we should return
the liquor traffic to America in any form whatsoever, our
liquor bill would be practically double what it was before
the war. The natural increase in prices would alone
assure this. The cost of the liquor trade has practically
doubled in every country where it is still licensed. Let
every American citizen think what that would mean to
business. Our annual income as a nation is probably not
more than forty billion dollars. Prohibition rescues one
eighth of our annual income for business. You know that
your own business or your father's business could not stand
the loss of one eighth of its annual inflow. It is the last
twelve per cent of business that makes the profit. The first
seven eighths take care of salaries and overhead. The last
eighth provides the profit that is invested to build more
factories, produce more goods, provide more employment,
add to the national wealth, and maintain educational and

philanthropic institutions. It is simply a matter of "life's margins." The packer does not make his chief profit on meat; he makes it on hides, hair, horns, bone. In this day of all days we cannot stand the waste of a five-billion-dollar drink bill. We have been speaking only of the direct cost of the liquor traffic. There was a vast consequential cost imposed upon the nation by increased crime, pauperism, and other evils of the trade. Expert economists believe that this cost was as great as the direct cost.

What this waste means to the world.—Savings must save the world. The crux of the world problem to-day is economic. If Europe could put a stop to its expenditures either for military establishments or for alcohol, there would be no serious economic problems, and the greater relief would come from the cessation of the traffic in drink. For instance, France in 1921 spent thirteen and a half billion francs for alcoholic liquor. French expenditures for the army and navy although not accurately known at present, were not more than five billion francs. At any rate it is certain that the sum for such purposes was far below the drink expenditure. Switzerland, Holland, Great Britain, Belgium, Germany, and Austria are spending not much less than five billion dollars annually for intoxicants—far more than they are spending for education or even for bread and milk, and enormously more than they are spending on wasteful military establishments. In the words of *The Case for Prohibition:*

Prohibition stands shoulder to shoulder with peace as the twin giants which can solve the world's problems. The spectacular character of the great waste of war, the fact that its waste is principally crowded into a few short, hectic years, drives home to the conviction of the world the truth that if war could be banished, all other problems might be solved. But the drink evil is very nearly as great a drain on the wealth and life of the world as war. When the guns were thundering on the western front, Lloyd George said, "We are fighting three enemies—Germany, Austria, and drink; and to my mind drink is the greatest of the three." It was literally true. If Great Britain and the other allied countries could have banished the evil of alcoholism for the period of the war, victory over Germany and Austria would have been assured without the intervention of the United States.

A cancer is none the less dangerous to life because it does

not act with the speed of the destructive lightning bolt. War is the lightning bolt, but drink is the cancer. It spreads its murder over the years and scatters its waste from generation to generation.

Sir George Paish, one of the leading economists of England, said:

"Prohibition is an economic question. There are two reasons for this. First, we must admit the working classes will command, from now on, a greater share of the world's goods than they have been getting before. Secondly, the difficulty of securing capital from the classes that formerly supplied capital will be exceedingly difficult because of taxes and fear of the future. Therefore, unless the working people make savings and provide capital, world business will be at a standstill. They can only make savings by denying themselves indulgences, which include drink. In England to-day they spend from 400,000,000 pounds to 500,000,000 pounds on drink. If half that amount were saved in England and elsewhere among the nations, the problems of the world would be solved. As an economist I consider prohibition is necessary and inevitable."

QUESTIONS FOR DISCUSSION

Do you believe that it pays to do right? If so, does it pay a nation as well as an individual?

Has labor any legitimate grievance against business because business favors prohibition for selfish reasons?

In your opinion can sober labor be trusted to get its fair share of prohibition benefits?

Suppose prohibition comes to your city. For the first time savings in the local bank greatly increase. This means more money for loans. Will that mean increased building? If so, what kind of structures? Will it mean more employment of labor at higher wages? Will it mean more consumption of raw materials? If so, will that again mean labor employment?

In your opinion what is the relation between abundance of capital and public morals?

A young man is reared in a home of great poverty. A friend is reared in a home of wealth. Has either one enjoyed the best environment? What constitutes the degree of comfort most conducive to good citizenship? Just how is prohibition a factor here?

What is the connection between prosperity and peace? If prohibition makes the average man prosperous does it make him dread disturbed conditions?

How many factors are there in the indirect cost of the liquor traffic? What would be the average cost to every family if the liquor traffic should return?

What is the relation between decreased immigration and the necessity for increased efficiency on the part of labor?

Woe unto them that join house to house, that lay field to field, till there be no room, and ye be made to dwell alone in the midst of the land! In mine ears *saith* Jehovah of hosts, Of a truth many houses shall be desolate, even great and fair, without inhabitant. For ten acres of vineyard shall yield one bath, and a homer of seed shall yield *but* an ephah. Woe unto them that rise up early in the morning, that they may follow strong drink; that tarry late into the night, till wine inflame them! And the harp and the lute, the tabret and the pipe, and the wine, are *in* their feasts; but they regard not the work of Jehovah, neither have they considered the operation of his hands.

Therefore my people are gone into captivity for lack of knowledge; and their honorable men are famished, and their multitude are parched with thirst. Therefore Sheol hath enlarged its desire, and opened its mouth without measure; and their glory, and their multitude, and their pomp, and he that rejoiceth among them, descend *into it*. And the mean man is bowed down, and the great man is humbled, and the eyes of the lofty are humbled: But Jehovah of hosts is exalted in justice, and God the Holy One is sanctified in righteousness. Then shall the lambs feed as in their pasture, and the waste places of the fat ones shall wanderers eat.

Woe unto them that draw iniquity with cords of falsehood, and sin as it were with a cart rope; that say, Let him make speed, let him hasten his work, that we may see it; and let the counsel of the Holy One of Israel draw nigh and come, that we may know it! Woe unto them that call evil good, and good evil; that put darkness for light, and light for darkness; that put bitter for sweet, and sweet for bitter! Woe unto them that are wise in their own eyes, and prudent in their own sight! Woe unto them that are mighty to drink wine, and men of strength to mingle strong drink; that justify the wicked for a bribe, and take away the righteousness of the righteous from him!

Therefore as the tongue of fire devoureth the stubble, and as the dry grass sinketh down in the flame, so their root shall be as rottenness, and their blossom shall go up as dust; because they have rejected the law of Jehovah of hosts, and despised the word of the Holy One of Israel. (Isa. 5. 8-24.)

CHAPTER VIII

DRINK IN POLITICS

The end of government is the welfare of mankind.—*Locke.*
Give me a sober population, not wasting their earnings in
strong drink, and I shall know where to obtain the revenues.
—*William E. Gladstone.*

IT is misleading to say that prohibition is an effort to
change the private habits of the people. It is an effort to
deal with the public problems arising not only from private
habits of drinkers but from the system of production and
distribution which supplied and intensified the appetite.
The problem of individual drunkenness, but for the character of the commodity, might have been met by moral suasion.
The social and political problems arising from the trade,
but for that same character of the commodity handled,
might also have been solved by other measures than prohibition. A poisonous and enslaving commodity, destroying
the free will of the individual, made continuation of the
free-trade policy of early days impossible. But most of
the public problems were created by the very efforts of the
government to control an evil institution through measures
short of stern repression.

THE EVOLUTION OF THE SALOON

The license system.—Regulation by license, repression
by taxation, produced the saloon. As we saw in Chapter
III, license meant on the part of the government permission, protection, and promotion. On the part of the
saloon and the liquor trade it directly produced an alliance
with predatory interests such as vice; with political
machines subsisting upon a corrupt vote; and with interests
depending on special favors from politicians because they
lacked natural and common-law rights. License compelled
the trade to coordinate its activities and concentrate its
power. The political influence of the brewers and dis-

tillers and the vile character of the saloon may be traced
to the license system.

The brewers' organization.—The United States Brewers'
Association was organized in the same year the federal
liquor-revenue act was passed. It faced the necessity of
raising the license money required by the government, and
that without seriously interfering with profits. It was en-
couraged by the fact that license had given it a new re-
spectability. The number of breweries and distilleries was
quickly reduced, and those remaining were strongly
established. Eventually about 85 per cent of the saloons
fell into the hands of the brewers, and every saloon was
not only a trade institution but also a political agency. The
very first meeting of the United States Brewers' Association organized a lobby. The per-capita consumption of
alcoholic liquors was forced by this closely organized trade
from a little more than two gallons in 1863 to about
twenty-three gallons in the last year before prohibition.

How the liquor traffic corrupted government.—The
systematic way in which this vast interest attempted control of government is almost unbelievable to this prohibition generation. A Senate committee of investigation,
just before prohibition, declared that the Brewers' Association had corrupted politics by the use of vast sums of
money; had secretly subsidized writers not generally known
to be connected with them and controlled newspapers; had
directed the machinery of racial organizations; had established an alliance with disloyal and semidisloyal groups;
had systematically organized a boycott of dry business men
and had used vast sums of money in violation of law. A
lobby was maintained in Washington. The agent in charge
of the legislative interests of the brewers was paid a salary
of forty thousand dollars annually. In Pittsburgh leading
brewers accepted a fine of nearly seventy thousand dollars
rather than allow to be produced in court testimony that
would have made the greatest scandal in the history of
the republic. In 1914 the United States Brewers' Association turned over to its legislative agent $330,138, and the
Wholesale Liquor Dealers' Association paid him $90,000
more. His only activities were political in nature. In the
same year, according to partial records confiscated by the

government, the Brewers' Association made collections aggregating $999,300.88. Other vast sums were spent through agents connected with racial organizations. To handicap investigation the brewers destroyed most of their records. Do you think we should give these same men a monopoly of the liquor business in America by once again permitting the sale of beer while prohibiting the sale of whisky?

The brewers and the saloon.—Everyone condemns the saloon. Even the wets pretend that they think its abolition a blessing. The saloon was not more corrupt than the organized brewers. But its corruption was closer to the people and more generally observed. That corruption should be charged to the brewers themselves; for the saloon keeper, oftener than eight times in ten, was simply an agent of the brewers, placed in the saloon under contract to sell a certain make of beer and under obligation to carry out the political instructions given him. The saloon brought the creation of a demand to a fine art. It harbored vice upstairs and gambling in the rear rooms; for these also were special privileges, and the alliance was a source of political strength.

A community center.—In cities overwhelmed with immigrants the saloon was a racial community center. In a German community it would be run by August; in a Scandinavian community by Ole; in an Irish community by Mike. Perhaps from 100 to 150 men a day would drop in to drink, play pinochle, and "visit." When one of these men lost his job, the saloon keeper would notify the political organization, and he would be put to sweeping the streets or would be given some other way of making a living. When his baby was sick, the political organization would be notified by the saloon keeper and it would furnish a doctor. When his baby died, the political organization would make a loan to enable him to bury the body and nine times out of ten it would collect the loan from the man's employer. The saloon keeper was always ready to extend credit to a "regular." When election time rolled around, the saloon keeper would pass the word to all these "regulars," to every man under an obligation, to every man with whom he had established an influence by alliance or otherwise. There was never another such political power. It extended from the top, represented by the brewers' organization, through all the avenues of life, by the use of the saloon.

THE LICENSE EVIL

What the government got out of it.—The federal government received a few hundred millions in tax money. The States and local communities received more. The American people "got" a liquor bill in excess of two billion dollars a year, inflicting upon them in addition injury that, so far as it can be estimated in money, amounted to as much more. And, after all, who paid the liquor tax? The brewers and distillers? Not one cent of it. Drinkers and their victims paid it. Those who drank the hardest paid the most tax. It was paid by women bending over the washtub, by the young man taking his first drink, by the reeling drunkard who had lost everything that a normal man holds dear. Do you think it paid?

Did the license system have any good points?—The argument is frequently offered that opening the saloons to sell beer would stop the illicit trade in liquors. There is nothing whatever to justify such a contention. We have bootleggers and we have blind pigs but we had them before prohibition. The retail license imposed by the federal government was small, most of the revenue being collected at the source of production. Consequently, illicit retail dealers, though avoiding the State and local taxes, usually paid the federal tax. In 1914 the Methodist Board of Temperance obtained reliable figures from a number of States in order to ascertain how many of these illicit dealers were revealed by the disparity between the numbers of federal and local license holders. It found that in Michigan there were 3,204 blind pigs. In New York there were 23,472 saloons licensed by the State, while the revenue tax had been paid by 34,522 persons. In Illinois there were just about as many blind pigs and bootleggers as there were saloons—10,046 to be exact—while in Kansas there were no saloons and only 515 purchasers of the federal license.

Shall we rescue the license system?—The advocates of

beer are inviting us back to the license system, to brewery organization, and to the saloon or some method of liquor distribution which would create just as evil an institution as the saloon. Let us not pass this subject without understanding clearly what these institutions which desire to return to our life were.

The saloon as conducted is a nuisance—a loafing place for the idle and vicious [acknowledged the *Wine and Spirit Gazette* of August 23, 1902]. It is generally on a prominent street and is run by a sport who cares only for the almighty dollar. From this resort the drunken man starts reeling home. At this resort the local fights are indulged in. It is a stench in the nostrils of society.

"Any man who knows the saloons well can honestly say that most of them have forfeited their right to live," said the *Wholesalers' and Retailers' Review* of September, 1907. "There is not a licensed saloon keeper in Illinois who does not lay himself liable to prosecution a dozen times a day," confessed the *Champion of Fair Play*, June 7, 1902.

Self-indicted.—Many similar indictments of the saloon from the lips of the trade itself could be given. Judge Kenesaw M. Landis, in commenting upon the professed intention of the brewers to clean up the saloons, called attention to the fact that the Anheuser-Busch Brewing Association controlled thirty-two of the worst saloons in East Saint Louis. He said:

I see that Mr. August A. Busch made a public statement bemoaning the fact that lawless saloon keepers have been responsible for antisaloon sentiment. Here are thirty-two saloons confessedly managed by Mr. Busch's company, and they have been steadfastly breaking the law for at least ten years.

Timothy McDonough, president of the National Liquor League, on May 13, 1911, referring to these same professions on the part of the brewers, said, "The resolutions of the brewers sound well but they are all rot."

A social degenerate.—The truth is that the saloon was a political and industrial degenerate, a pervert, a satisfier of no healthy human desire, no normal appetite. Its crimes were brutally simian, its strength the strength of the gorilla, its intelligence the cunning of the ape. And we allowed this degenerate to rule over us, dominate political parties, nominate candidates, name judges, seat aldermen, make mayors, define policies, stand whip in hand at our polls and in the lobbies of our State Legislatures!

THE STORY OF PROHIBITION

How temperance sentiment was shaped by circumstance. —It is frequently contended that prohibition was suddenly put over on the country; the truth is, however, that it was a gradual development—a development extending over a hundred years—and that temperance sentiment gradually shaped itself to the necessities of the case. When there was free trade in liquors, the resulting evils were of such a nature as to prompt the organization of temperance societies. At first these temperance societies were very mild in their suggestions. They advised a sparing use of liquor. They imposed a fine of twenty-five cents for drunkenness except (in the case of one society) "on the fourth of July or a regularly appointed military muster day." It was thought that encouragement of the manufacture and use of beer would discourage drunkenness. Finally this was found to be a fallacy, and total-abstinence societies arose. Then our fathers began to question the wisdom of granting a special privilege to a trade that produced such manifest evils. They favored high license in order to restrict these evils at least. Observing with alarm the rise of new wickedness under the influence of high license, they proposed that local communities have the privilege of entirely suppressing the trade when desired.

Local option and State prohibition.—Local option relieved many communities from the nuisance of the saloon but it could not be called an adequate remedy when saloons existed only a few miles or a few hundred feet away, and there was nothing to prevent importation of liquors into the communities without saloons. In States where the majority of the people became convinced that entire suppression of the traffic was the only remedy, State prohibition laws were passed. At first these were not strong laws but gradually they were made very drastic, and under them many States experienced splendid relief. But the day came when the liquor traffic adjusted itself somewhat to State prohibition, building up a great mail-order business over State boundaries, reaping profits for itself, and playing havoc with the public peace in dry communities.

The prohibitionists win Congress.—Congress had already recognized temperance sentiment by suppressing the saloon in the Capitol building, by abolishing the army canteen, and similar measures; but it was not until March 1, 1913, that prohibitionists demonstrated that they had an actual majority in Congress. On that date the so-called Webb-Kenyon law, prohibiting the transportation of liquors in interstate commerce into prohibition States was enacted. A long series of important prohibition laws preceded the submission of the constitutional amendment, and it is hard to see how the wets can claim that they were taken by surprise. In 1917 a prohibition law was passed for Alaska at the request of that territory. In the same year the Porto Ricans voted for prohibition, and in deference to that vote Congress passed a prohibition law for them. Almost on the same day Congress made the nation's capital dry. The interstate trade in liquors had become such a scandal that the Randall amendment to the Post Office Appropriations Bill barred liquor advertising from the mails and absolutely prohibited the transportation of liquors into any territory that was under prohibition.

The influence of the war.—At this time the world was wrapped in the flames of war, and it was becoming evident that the intervention of the United States must be made real and effective if the war was to be brought to an end with the least danger to our freedom and interests. The act increasing the military establishment of the United States protected the nation's soldiers from the evil of drink by establishing dry zones around camps. Later in the year the Food Control Act, to prevent the waste of foodstuffs, empowered the President to suppress the malting of grain for beer manufacture. Meanwhile prohibitionists were becoming impatient. They had a vast majority in Congress, elected in hundreds of election contests in which prohibition had been a dominant issue. They felt that the people had expressed their will in the election of these men, so they forced a vote on the submission of the prohibition amendment to the Constitution and won by votes to spare over the two-thirds majority required. Meanwhile the war raged. Thousands of bushels of grain and tons of sugar were still being used to produce intoxicating liquors, while mothers were being begged to eat less bread and to be careful of the crumbs. The conscience of the country was disturbed. It was felt that the boys in uniform would not be properly supported until every food resource of the nation was being conserved for victory. So, despite the fact that the prohibition amendment had been submitted, the war-prohibition act, to become effective in a short time, was passed. In 1919 the prohibition amendment, which had been ratified, was supported by a prohibition-enforcement act. Constitutional prohibition became effective January 16, 1920, and up to this time has had the support of the Legislatures of forty-six of the forty-eight States. The will of the people has been written into the charter of American liberties, and the government is forbidden to grant a special privilege that is abhorrent to natural rights, inimical to the general welfare, a peril to the common defense, and a travesty upon justice.

QUESTIONS FOR DISCUSSION

What are some of the public aspects of the drink problem?

What is the effect upon the government of any recognition whatsoever of the liquor trade? What are some of the effects upon the liquor trade itself?

Do you think the political corruption proceeding from the Brewers' Association was inevitable under the license system?

How did the saloon build political influence upon racial appeal?

In what sense was the saloon a club? In what sense a charitable organization?

Is it possible to make the liquor trade a financial asset to the government?

Would a return to the license system banish bootlegging and blind pigs?

In the light of the gradual development of the temperance movement what about the argument that prohibition was suddenly put over?

Why was local option an imperfect policy?

Why should not the States be allowed to handle the liquor traffic as they please?

How much warning was afforded the liquor people by the final development of the national prohibition movement?

Let every soul be in subjection to the higher powers: for there is no power but of God; and the *powers* that be are ordained of God. Therefore he that resisteth the power, withstandeth the ordinance of God: and they that withstand shall receive to themselves judgment. For rulers are not a terror to the good work, but to the evil. And wouldest thou have no fear of the power? do that which is good, and thou shalt have praise from the same: for he is a minister of God to thee for good. But if thou do that which is evil, be afraid; for he beareth not the sword in vain: for he is a minister of God, an avenger for wrath to him that doeth evil. Wherefore ye must needs be in subjection, not only because of the wrath but also for conscience' sake. For this cause ye pay tribute also; for they are ministers of God's service attending continually upon this very thing. Render to all their dues; tribute to whom tribute *is due*; custom to whom custom; fear to whom fear; honor to whom honor. (Rom. 13. 1-7.)

CHAPTER IX

THE BIRTH OF A NEW POLICY

But the worst of all . . . is the systematic alcoholizing of mankind on the strength of a bad custom, which is old enough, to be sure, but which has become an acute pestilence in our modern civilization.—*Dr. August Forel, University of Zurich.*

PSYCHOLOGISTS tell us that we do many things to-day because our ancestors did them five thousand years ago. When you shake hands with your friend you use your right hand because that is the one that might hold a weapon. Possibly you have two buttons on the back of your coat. A hundred years ago such buttons were supposed to hold the sword belt in place. We don't need them to-day, but the tailors keep putting them on just the same.

So drink had established itself in the customs of the race. We had the habit of the saloon. We had the habit of serving liquors at our entertainments, of treating. All the suggestion of our literature was to the effect that drinking was a social act, that wine warmed the heart and stimulated the flow of good cheer. Many motion pictures give us that same literary suggestion to-day. We find it in the newspapers and in popular songs. In the words of Dr. Clarence True Wilson, "Prohibition has had only five years to overcome a habit five thousand years old." Possibly you have habits of your own which are hard to control. The race has just as much trouble in handling its bad habits, especially so because many thousands of people act as tempters, striving earnestly to perpetuate the drink habit, to continue its hold upon society, literature, and song.

Prohibition destroyed much of the financial interest in the drink habit but not all of it. For instance, the brewers who make near beer to-day do so by making beer and then steaming out the alcohol. This of course adds to the cost of the operation, and they long for the old days when the manufacture of beer was a simple matter, and profits were large.

Many banks lent money to distillers who had whisky in bonded warehouses, taking warehouse certificates as collateral. These certificates greatly declined in value after prohibition, and many of these banks would like to see a return of the unhampered drink trade in order to increase the value of this collateral on which they have lent money. In several cities banks so interested are closely connected with newspapers, and we find the newspapers bitterly fighting the prohibition law.

SOME ENFORCEMENT DIFFICULTIES

Political influence upon appointments.—When the Volstead law was enacted, many people doubted the wisdom of placing them under civil service. It was thought that perhaps men who were opposed to the prohibition law might get civil-service appointment as prohibition agents, and that they could not be so easily discharged from their positions if they proved unfit. By leaving the appointment of agents a political matter it was believed that the senator or congressman who obtained the appointment could be held responsible for the character of the man he named. This has not worked out well. For example, a senator such as the senator from New Jersey, who is opposed to prohibition enforcement, might recommend an agent utterly unfit for the position; and the fact that the drys were displeased with his recommendation would mean nothing to the senator, as he depended on the wets for his election. Even senators who voted for the prohibition law have made bad recommendations without the fact seeming to have come to the attention of their constituencies at all. Undoubtedly many utterly unfit agents were appointed; but it is also undoubtedly true that many of these have been gradually weeded out as they have been found unfit. The placing of appointments under civil service, while it promises to work an improvement in conditions, will not entirely eliminate political influence.

Liquors remaining in bond.—Under the license system it was required of distillers that every gallon of whisky produced must be kept in a warehouse under government supervision. The distiller did not have to pay the tax on this whisky until it was withdrawn for sale or other consumption. When prohibition went into effect, there were millions of gallons of such whisky in government warehouses. In lieu of compensation Congress had allowed the liquor dealers one year's notice. The prohibition law did not go into effect until one year after its final approval. Of course, the persons who wished to store liquors for future consumption immediately began to lay in their stores, and the price of whisky went to a very high point. Nevertheless, the overproduction had been so great that the warehouses contained millions of gallons in storage. Of course, after prohibition the bootleggers began to use their wits to get this liquor out of the warehouses and into the bootleg trade. It was stored at many different points, and the warehouses were poorly guarded. Sometimes the guards would be rushed, and the warehouses robbed. Sometimes it was evident that there was collusion between the guards and the robbers. Counterfeit permits were frequently offered at warehouses, and liquor was withdrawn before the forgery was discovered. Whisky being transported in trucks was stolen by highwaymen. The government undertook to solve these difficulties immediately. A special paper, making the forgery of permits very difficult, was prepared. Congress provided for the concentration of liquors in a relatively small number of warehouses, which could be well guarded. The transportation of liquors by automobile was stopped. It is probable that now almost no bonded liquors are escaping from the government warehouses to the bootleggers. Less than two million gallons of bonded whisky annually is being consumed by the American people, and all of this is needed for purposes legitimate under the law. Before prohibition the American people were using approximately 150,000,000 gallons of liquor annually.

The rise and fall of home brew.—Evasion of the prohibition law also took the direction of an attempt to make liquors, principally beer, at home. Manufacturers began to advertise beer materials designed for such home production, and for a short time such materials were generally on sale even in the most unexpected places. But the evil was not persistent because of the fact that the making of beer is a delicate operation, and the messes produced by novices were not only exceedingly unwholesome and unpalatable but gave off a vile odor. To-day very little material for the manufacture of beer is sold for home use. In our largest cities it is possible to locate a few small stores that specialize in such goods. The lawless temperament of these people is also clearly indicated by the sale of apparatus that is obviously intended for law violation. Broadly speaking, however, it may be said that home brew to-day is hardly a factor in the problem of prohibition enforcement. This is admitted by such leading wets as Hugh Fox, one-time secretary of the United States Brewers' Association. In New York and other large cities there is a great deal of manufacture by immigrants of wine for personal use, particularly by Italians and Greeks. It must be remembered, however, that these people always consumed large quantities of wine, and it is probable that they are not consuming anything like as much as they did before the law stopped importation and the organized manufacture and distribution of liquor.

Smuggling from the sea.—Another problem requiring the immediate attention of the federal government was the stopping of illicit importation of liquors, particularly Scotch whisky. Such importation never equaled the liquor importation before prohibition, not to speak of the vast domestic manufacture. It is impossible to estimate with a fair degree of accuracy the extent of this smuggling because most of these shipments of liquors originated in the British Isles. They were shipped direct to the United States or transported to Canada, Mexico, and the West Indies with a view to their eventual sale in the States. Great Britain kept a very accurate record of the amount of liquor leaving the British Isles for these countries, and the records substantiate the statement above made. The entire exportation from Great Britain and Canada in 1924 was only 4,186,468 gallons, while our domestic production before prohibition was usually about 150,000,000 gallons. It is probable that the yearly importation by smuggling rarely exceeded two million gallons.

But there was a feature of this nuisance which made it highly important that the United States should deal with it effectively. The smugglers, approaching the American coast off the large cities, particularly New York, took their stations just beyond the three-mile limit, where they were visited by small fast craft from the shore. Their presence within sight of American land, engaged as they were in promoting violation of American law, constituted an affront little short of an act of war.

SOLVING ENFORCEMENT PROBLEMS

A treaty with Great Britain.—The American people became more and more irritated. The British people became more and more humiliated. They did not approve of this illicit trade. Indeed, their papers unanimously and vigorously denounced it. Nevertheless, some of their leading men, even of title, engaged in it openly. Obviously something must be done. So the American government approached Great Britain with a proposition that American authority to search and seize be extended to twelve miles from the American shore, or one hour's sail. By holding the smugglers at this distance the United States officials were better able to run down and capture the small fast boats that supplied their connection with the shore. The treaty was ratified by Great Britain and the United States, and similar treaties were effected with other countries.

The use of naval vessels.—Then Congress became determined that adequate means should be furnished for suppression of the smugglers. Conclusion of the recent war had left the United States with an oversupply of destroyers. A score of these were transferred to the Coast Guard. Nearly three hundred other vessels, some of them fast and small for close-inshore work, were also provided. Using the new weapons, the Coast Guard quickly suppressed the smugglers and reduced the importation from the sea to a trickle. Whisky still comes across the Canadian and Mexican borders, but the government has also undertaken suppression of this smuggling and is getting praiseworthy results.

Reorganizing the prohibition unit.—The first organization for prohibition enforcement was characterized by many faults. John F. Kramer, the first Prohibition Commissioner, was an earnest dry but found himself greatly hampered by the lack of precedent and organization. He was succeeded by Major Roy A. Haynes, a Methodist and a prohibitionist; but Mr. Haynes operated under the Commissioner of Internal Revenue, who was under an assistant to the Secretary of the Treasury, who was under the Secretary of the Treasury himself. The Secretary of the Treasury was not a prohibitionist; indeed, he had at one time been interested in the manufacture of whisky. The commissioner had little authority. It was hard for him to cooperate with the customs force and the Coast Guard, which was supposed to suppress smuggling. Also, he found himself hampered by the fact that it was the duty of the Prohibition Unit only to prepare cases. They must be prosecuted by the district attorneys, many of whom were wet, and tried before judges, many of whom were also wet. In an effort to overcome some of the difficulties President Coolidge concentrated authority in the hands of General Lincoln Andrews, who was made an Assistant Secretary of the Treasury and who was given a free hand by the Secretary. The customs and the Coast Guard forces were also put under Andrews' direction. It was felt that the general, who was in close touch with officials in the Department of Justice, would be able to coordinate the various forces, to cooperate with the Justice Department effectively, and to get the best results. General Andrews adopted the policy of decentralization; that is, he divided the country into districts, appointed a prohibition administrator for each district, gave him full authority to employ his own agents, and held him responsible for *results*. He announced that he would not consider politics in making these appointments, that he would seek men who wished to be of service to their country and who were willing to serve at a sacrifice. It is fair to say that he has not been able to carry out his plan.

Controlling industrial alcohol.—The greatest problem facing General Andrews to-day is that of control of the manufacture and distribution of industrial alcohol. Alcohol is used in the manufacture of flavoring extracts, medicines, perfumes, barber supplies, and scores of other things, even including the making of hairbrushes and felt hats. Due to the taking over by American industry of certain German trades during the war and to the natural expansion of American business the use of alcohol for these legitimate purposes has enormously increased. The government has desired to make the legitimate use of alcohol easy and convenient but has been faced with the problem of the diversion of alcohol issued to the legitimate trade. To safeguard its use much of the industrial alcohol is denatured; that is, substances are added which make it unfit for human consumption. But bootleggers who succeed in diverting this alcohol redistill it, thus partially freeing the product from much of the distasteful or poisonous matter. They then color it, put it into bottles ornamented by false labels and revenue stamps, and sell it as "good" whisky. This kind of liquor is the chief supply of the bootleg trade in Eastern cities. Much of it is thought by consumers to be Scotch or prewar bottled liquors. It is important to know that bootleg methods of redistillation cannot eliminate entirely denaturants which are poisonous or injurious. There is a lack of sufficient legislation to deal with this problem adequately, and no doubt Congress will amend the law in order to strengthen the hands of the Treasury.

Dealing with the moonshiner.—There is of course the ever-present moonshiner, who produces "corn liquor." The quantity produced by such moonshiners is generally greatly overestimated. Usually their stills are small, and they are not in operation long before seizure. Sometimes, however, in particularly lawless sections or communities large stills operate. It is doubtful, however, whether all of the moonshine product equals the output of one of the large distilleries of Peoria or Louisville—plants that sometimes used thousands of bushels of corn daily. Young people should know the horrible character of "shine." Practically all of it is produced under conditions of unspeakable filth. It would be easy to supply details if they were not too revolting. Of course, the success of the moonshiner's effort depends largely on the speed with which he produces his product. Every hour adds to his danger. Consequently, almost all of them add to the mash certain material that heats it quickly but which is fit only for fertilizing purposes.

Strengthening local agencies.—Even States where prohibition sentiment is strongest have, since national prohibition, shown a tendency to throw the entire burden of enforcement on the federal government. This is wrong in principle and disastrous in consequences. The federal government was not designed primarily to do police work, most of which properly falls upon the State and municipality. The federal government should deal with the federal problems of liquor enforcement, and citizens should see that the State and local police suppress the small moonshiner and bootlegger. The local governments are closer to the people than the federal government, and individual officers can be held to responsibility at the polls much more effectively. Satisfactory enforcement will be impossible until our people realize these things.

The citizen's duty.—One by one many difficulties facing the federal government have been dealt with and overcome, and remaining problems will be dealt with as the days pass. There is a necessity of coordinated action in favor of prohibition on the part of all legislative, judicial, and executive offices. Our political position in so far as it depends on elections is strong, but many executive and judicial officers are not giving proper support to the law. The people should insist that they do so.

QUESTIONS FOR DISCUSSION

What are some national habits as distinct from habits of the individual?

Tell some ways in which the drink habit still handicaps the enforcement of prohibition.

Why does a senator who votes dry sometimes recommend wet prohibition agents?

How did the "one year's grace" provision serve to compensate the whisky interests?

How can the government better solve the problem of handling bonded liquors?

Name some other prohibition problems that have been effectively dealt with by the government.

What are some problems which remain to be solved?

Does your State enforce the prohibition law?

If not, do prohibitionists of your State insist that it do so, or do they depend on the federal government?

When the righteous are increased, the people rejoice;
But when a wicked man beareth rule, the people sigh.

The king by justice establisheth the land;
But he that exacteth gifts overthroweth it.

The king that faithfully judgeth the poor,
His throne shall be established for ever.
The rod and reproof give wisdom;
But a child left to himself causeth shame to his mother.
When the wicked are increased, transgression increaseth;
But the righteous shall look upon their fall.
Correct thy son, and he will give thee rest;
Yea, he will give delight unto thy soul.
Where there is no vision, the people cast off restraint;
But he that keepeth the law, happy is he.
A servant will not be corrected by words;
For though he understand, he will not give heed.

The fear of man bringeth a snare;
But whoso putteth his trust in Jehovah shall be safe.
                              (Prov. 29. 2, 4, 14-19, 25.)

CHAPTER X

IN THE FOOTSTEPS OF STATESMEN

Like so many boxes of Pandora dramshops are hourly scattering plagues of every kind—natural, moral, and political. The worst effect of all—and which ought to make every man who has the least sense of his privilege tremble—these houses are become in many places the nurseries of our legislators. . . . I think it would be well worth the attention of our Legislature to confine the number and retrieve the character of licensed houses, lest that impiety and profaneness, that abandoned intemperance and prodigality, that impudence and brawling temper, which these abominable nurseries daily propagate, should arrive at last to a degree of strength that even the Legislature will not be able to control.—*President John Adams.*

"OTHER times, other manners." In America we do not suffer from the curse of ancestor worship. What was good enough for father may not be good enough for us; and recognition of the fact implies no disrespect to the generations gone. Antiprohibitionists often quote some of the men to whom the country is most indebted as favoring— or, at least, not condemning—the sale and consumption of alcoholic liquors. Washington, we are told, was a distiller; Lincoln a saloon keeper; Jefferson an ardent advocate of wine and beer as a solution of the liquor problem.

What did Washington know of the modern scientific revelations as to the character of alcohol? What did Jefferson know of the modern beer trade, which corrupted politicians, intimidated city and State governments, harbored vice, and exploited the unfortunate? Just as the entire teaching of Christ's life was contrary to the toleration of an organized liquor traffic, filling the streets with temptation, so the lives of the patriots of the early days justify us in the belief that most of them, if not all of them, would be prohibitionists to-day. We must apply the fundamental principles that governed their lives to the problems of this day in the same spirit in which they applied them, often with limited information, to the problems of their own day. The fathers advanced the common welfare as the supreme law of the land, just as Jesus Christ advanced brotherhood as the law of the Kingdom. Under this principle the common welfare can be protected and fostered, and whatever endangers it may be prohibited and abolished. The dead hand of the past cannot bind the present. Nor does the fact that wrong was once permitted constitute an indictment of an age that strove earnestly toward the light. The great precedents of history call for the overthrow of wrong when it has been discovered.

The First President and Drink

In advance of his day.—What is the meaning of George Washington's life to the young men and young women of to-day? Washington was not a prohibitionist. He made liquor and he consumed liquor, yet he was "first in war, first in peace, and first in the hearts of his countrymen." The significant fact is that he was in advance of the sentiment of the eighteenth century. When drunkenness was common and "gentlemanly," he was never drunk. When excess was nearly universal, he was moderate. He was as far in advance of the sentiment of his day as the radical prohibitionist was in advance of the sentiment of 1910. On more than one occasion he showed a lively realization of the evil nature of alcohol and tried to suppress its consumption.

General Washington's order.—On May 26, 1778, he issued an order directing that a corporal and eight men, with the commissary of each brigade, should be detailed to confiscate the liquors found in tippling houses in the vicinity of his camp, and also that they should notify the inhabitants "or persons living in the vicinity of camp that an unconditional seizure will be made of all liquors they shall presume to sell in the future." Once again, he issued this prohibition:

All persons whatever are forbid selling liquor to the Indians. If any sutler or soldier shall presume to act contrary to this prohibition, the former shall be dismissed from camp, and the latter receive severe corporal punishment.

PROHIBITION AND THE GREAT DEMOCRAT

Jefferson a temperance man.—Thomas Jefferson is frequently quoted to-day in support of the proposition to substitute the sale of wine and beer for prohibition, yet Jefferson was probably the most radical temperance man of his day. He asserted that whisky "kills one third of our citizens and ruins their families," and in order to minimize this evil he advised that breweries be established, and the people be exhorted to drink beer instead of whisky. He had had no experience either with the beer trade as afterward developed in this country or with the general consumption of beer. His fellow Americans were whisky drinkers, and no one living in that day dreamed of opposing the drinking of beer on the grounds of temperance. Jefferson advocated taxing the whisky business out of existence and was the first one to secure the passage of a national prohibitory law, which in that case applied to the Indians. His vivid recognition of the evils of whisky drinking, his signing of the prohibitory law (which indicates his conviction that prohibition, when advisable in practice, was not unjust as a principle), teach us that were he living to-day he would move to destroy the institutional evils of the liquor trade by drastic prohibitory measures.

HAMILTON AND FRANKLIN

Franklin's total abstinence.—Jefferson's great political antagonist—Alexander Hamilton—in the *Federalist* argued for repressive taxation of spirits. Benjamin Franklin boasted of his early total abstinence from both spirits and beer, being one of the few abstainers of the period. Speaking of his experience in the Watts Printing House, London, Franklin said:

I drank only water; other workmen, near fifty in number, were great guzzlers of beer. On occasion I carried up and downstairs a large form of type in each hand, when others carried but one in both hands. They wondered to see, from this and several instances, that the "water American," as they called me, was stronger than themselves who drank beer.

We had an alehouse boy who attended always in the house to supply the workmen. My companion at the press drank every day a pint before breakfast, a pint at breakfast with his bread and cheese, a pint between breakfast and dinner, a pint at dinner, and another when he had done his day's work. I thought it a detestable custom; but it was necessary, he supposed, to drink strong beer, that he might be strong in labor. I endeavored to convince him that the bodily strength afforded by beer could only be in proportion to the grain or flour of the barley dissolved in water of which it was made; that there was more flour in a pennyworth of bread; and, therefore, if he would eat that with a pint of water, it would give him more strength than a quart of beer. He drank on, however, and had four or five shillings to pay out of his wages every Saturday night for that muddling liquor: an expense I was free from. And thus these poor devils keep themselves always under.

ABRAHAM LINCOLN AND THE TRADE

Conflicting views.—Prohibitionists assert that Abraham Lincoln was a prohibitionist; antiprohibitionists say that he was opposed to prohibition, that he and his partner Berry sold liquors in their store, that while a legislator in Illinois in 1840 he voted against State prohibition and somewhat later against a local-option measure, that he himself drank upon several occasions.

A spurious statement.—The false statement most frequently attributed to Lincoln follows:

Prohibition will work great injury to the cause of temperance. It is a species of intemperance within itself, for it goes beyond the bounds of reason in that it attempts to control a man's appetite by legislation and in making crimes out of things that are not crimes. A prohibition law strikes a blow at the very principles on which our government was founded.

Lincoln never made this statement. In 1887, in Atlanta, Georgia, a local-option campaign was in progress. The colored people voted freely at that time in Atlanta, and the wets circulated among them a leaflet bearing this statement, followed by an appeal to vote wet. Hay and Nicolay, Lincoln biographers, denied that the quotation was authentic. Colonel T. M. Gilmore, distiller and head of the National Model License League, admitted, "As to the reported words of Abraham Lincoln on prohibition, beginning, 'Prohibition will work great injury to the cause of temperance,' I beg leave to say that I cannot at this time tell you where the original may be found." The Rev. Sam Small, of Atlanta, said that a man who led the fight against prohibition in the 1887 campaign admitted to him that the statement was a forgery.

Not in the whisky business.—It is true that a license was issued to Lincoln and Berry to sell liquors in their small grocery; but Miss Ida M. Tarbell, one of the greatest students of his life, says that his name was signed to the bond "by some other than himself, very likely by his partner" Berry, whose drinking habits caused the store to fail, thus imposing on Abraham Lincoln a debt that he called the greatest obstacle to his career. It was certain that the tavern license was never used. Leonard Swett, a Lincoln biographer, says that a controversy between Lincoln and his partner took place in regard to the introduction of whisky into the establishment. During most of the time when the store was in operation, Lincoln was absent in the Black Hawk War.

Lincoln the legislator.—Lincoln's votes in the Illinois Legislature may be easily explained. He voted against local option because it was a wet policy put forward in opposition to prohibition. He voted against State prohibition when such a measure was proposed by a liquor dealer in order to confuse a fight in progress for greater restrictions upon the liquor trade. His vote was of parliamentary significance only.

Lincoln an abstainer.—Arnold, in his life of Lincoln, says that "he used neither tobacco nor intoxicating drinks." Herndon quotes a companion as saying: "I am certain that he never drank intoxicating liquors. He did not even smoke or chew tobacco." John Hay, the great statesman and Lincoln biographer, says, "He made no use of either whisky or tobacco." Nicolay testifies, "I never saw him take a drink of whisky and never knew nor heard of his taking one." Similar testimony might be offered at great length, but it is unnecessary. We have Lincoln's own testimony, and there is no better. On January 19, 1838, he took the following pledge in connection with the Sangamon Temperance Society:

The members of this society agree not to use intoxicating liquor or provide it as an article of refreshment for their friends nor for persons in their employment, nor will they use, manufacture, or traffic in the same except for chemical, mechanical, medicinal, and sacramental purposes.

Lincoln added to his pledge "especially never to drink ardent spirits." He became a member of the Sons of Temperance and pledged himself "never to make, buy, sell, nor use as a beverage any spirituous or malt liquors, wine or cider," which definitely places him opposed to beer and wine as well as whisky.

Lincoln a prohibitionist.—Lincoln and George Edward Pickett, afterward a division commander in General Robert E. Lee's army, were the warmest of friends. This friendship began in Illinois, where Pickett had gone from Virginia to study law in the office of a kinsman. When Lincoln was elected to Congress he obtained through a friend an appointment for young Pickett to West Point. The close friendship formed in Illinois lasted without a break until Lincoln's death. When Richmond was burning, Mrs. Pickett, deserted by the servants, heard a knock at the door. Opening it, with her baby in her arms, she saw President Lincoln, who said, "I just came to see George Pickett's boy." While the young cadet was in West Point, Lincoln wrote to him:

I have just told the folks here in Springfield on this hundred and eleventh anniversary of the birth of him whose name was mightiest in the cause of civil law, in naked, deathless splendor, that the one victory we can ever call complete will be that one which proclaims that there is not one slave or drunkard on the face of God's green earth. Recruit for this victory!

"The temperance revolution."—On the twenty-second day of February, 1842, Lincoln addressed the Washingtonian Temperance Society, of Springfield, at the Second Presbyterian Church. In this address he said:

Turn now to the temperance revolution. In it we shall find a stronger bondage broken, a viler slavery manumitted, a greater tyrant deposed—in it, more of want supplied, more disease healed, more sorrow assuaged; by it, no orphans starving, no widows weeping; by it, none wounded in feeling, none injured in interest; even the drammaker and dramseller will have glided into other occupations so gradually as never to have felt the change and will stand ready to join all others in the universal song of gladness. And what a noble ally this to the cause of political freedom! With such an aid its march cannot fail to be on and on till every son of earth shall drink in rich fruition the sorrow-quenching drafts of perfect liberty. Happy day when all appetites controlled, all poisons subdued, all matter subjected! Mind, all conquering mind, shall live and move, the monarch of the world. Glorious consummation! Hail, fall of fury! Reign of reason, all hail!

And when the victory shall be complete—when there shall be neither a slave nor drunkard on the earth—how proud the title of that *Land*, which may truly claim to be the birthplace and the cradle of both those revolutions that shall have ended in that victory! How nobly distinguished that people, who shall have planted, and nurtured to maturity, both the political and moral freedom of their species!

"Sons of Temperance."—Lincoln assured a deputation of the Sons of Temperance waiting upon him on September 29, 1863, in behalf of the suppression of liquor-drinking in the Army, that they had his friendship and sympathy, his words being as follows:

If I were better known than I am, you would not need to be told that in the advocacy of the cause of temperance you have a friend and sympathizer in me. When I was a young man—long before the Sons of Temperance as an organization had an existence—I, in a humble way, made temperance speeches, and I think I may say that to this day I have never, by my example, belied what I then said. I think that the reasonable men of the world have long since agreed that intemperance is one of the greatest, if not the very greatest, of all evils among mankind. That is not a matter of dispute, I believe. That the disease exists, and that it is a very great one, is agreed upon by all. The mode of cure is one about which there may be differences of opinion. You have suggested that in an army—our army—drunkenness is a great evil, and one which, while it exists to a very great extent, we cannot expect to overcome so entirely as to have such successes in our arms as we might have without it. This undoubtedly is true, and while it is perhaps rather a bad source to derive comfort from, nevertheless in a hard struggle I do not know but what it is some consolation to be aware that there is some intemperance on the other side too; and that they have no right to beat us in physical combat on that ground.

A misquotation.—The unfair nature of liquor propaganda is indicated by one instance. The wets frequently quote Lincoln as having said that the injury done by liquor "did not arise from the use of a bad thing but the abuse of a very good thing." He was speaking of the fact that intemperance was universally acknowledged to be an evil, *"but none seemed to think"* that the injury arose from the use of a bad thing but from the abuse of a very good thing! What is to be thought of the honesty of such propaganda as this?

Lincoln's indorsement of prohibition.—On January 23, 1852, the Rev. James Smith, D.D., of Springfield, Illinois, delivered a temperance address in which he said:

> The liquor traffic is a cancer in society, eating out its vitals and threatening destruction, and all efforts to regulate it will not only prove abortive but will aggravate the evil. There must be no more effort to regulate the cancer; it must be eradicated. Not a root must be left; for until this is done, all classes must continue in danger of becoming victims of strong drink.

On the following day thirty-nine citizens, of whom Lincoln was one, presented to Doctor Smith a letter indorsing the address and urging that it be widely circulated.

In the Paths of the Fathers

The great men of the present day—men great in industry, men great in finance, great in education and politics—who advocate prohibition because they believe that it will eventually destroy one of the great scourges of the race are justified in believing that they tread in the paths of the fathers.

Questions for Discussion

How do you think the changed character of the liquor problem would affect George Washington's attitude toward it to-day?

What guiding principles in the lives of Washington, Jefferson, and others indicate what our attitude toward the liquor traffic should be?

Does the fact that Jefferson advocated the use of beer in his day indicate that his position would be the same now? Do you know anyone else of Jefferson's day who held a more advanced temperance position than he did?

Do you think Abraham Lincoln's abstinence from liquor

indicated that he was physically or mentally weak? Would he have been a stronger man if he had used intoxicants?

What is the significance of the fact that Lincoln coupled slavery and the drink evil in his thought? Did he expect to free the slaves without legislation? Is it reasonable to think he expected to free the country from saloons without law?

What is the moral obligation of a man who indorses the sentiments of another? Does he or does he not make them his sentiments?

But if any man buildeth on the foundation gold, silver, costly stones, wood, hay, stubble; each man's work shall be made manifest: for the day shall declare it, because it is revealed in fire; and the fire itself shall prove each man's work of what sort it is. If any man's work shall abide which he built thereon, he shall receive a reward. If any man's work shall be burned, he shall suffer loss: but he himself shall be saved; yet so as through fire.

Know ye not that ye are a temple of God, and *that* the Spirit of God dwelleth in you? If any man destroyeth the temple of God, him shall God destroy; for the temple of God is holy, and such are ye. (1 Cor. 3. 12-17.)

CHAPTER XI

THE QUESTION OF BEER AND WINE

It is my professional opinion, after observation of many years in the practice of medicine, that beer is doing more harm to humanity than all other alcoholics.

A man cannot use beer daily for any great length of time and not manifest some physiological deficiency.—*Dr. Gilbert Davis.*

Nothing is more erroneous from the physician's standpoint than to think of diminishing the destructive effects of alcoholism by substituting beer for other alcoholic drinks, or that the victims of drink are found only in those countries where whisky helps the people of a low grade of culture to forget their poverty and misery.—*Doctor Struempell.*

LLOYD GEORGE says that during all the time that he was in America he met no one who would vote for the return of the saloon. During the present generation America has known of only two methods of dealing with the liquor traffic. These two methods are license, with the saloon as the distributing agency, and prohibition. The opponents of prohibition therefore admit that prohibition is far better than the only other method of dealing with the traffic ever known to the American people. They propose that we undertake an experiment and they support their proposal by contending that this experiment has been successful in Europe and in Quebec. Their proposal is to license the liquor trade as before but to permit only the sale of so-called "light" wines and beer, and not to permit the sale of these in saloons.

ARE WINE AND BEER INTOXICATING?

The hope of the wets.—Let us remember that we are dealing with a certain commodity and a method of distributing it. The constitutional amendment, which no one contends can ever be overthrown, as it is just as hard to get it out as it was to get it into the Constitution, does not prohibit only the saloon: it prohibits the importation, exportation, manufacture, or sale of intoxicating liquors. The Volstead law is a statutory act passed under this constitutional amendment, which defines intoxicating liquors and gives to the executive and the judiciary instructions as to how the constitutional provision shall be carried out. Congress cannot pass a law permitting the sale of wines and beer if they are intoxicating, but the wets offer the entirely new contention that they are *not* intoxicating.

Wine intoxicating.—What are the facts? Simple fermentation gives to wine an alcohol content of thirteen per cent. Even if we were to admit—and it would be an absurd admission—that Frenchmen who drink wine do not become intoxicated, that would not alter the fact that the average man who drinks sufficient wine will become drunken.

A matter of quantity.—As to beer there is more latitude of opinion. Perhaps it would be nearly impossible for some men to become intoxicated on beer. As Dr. Clarence True Wilson well said, "Alcohol must go to the brain in order to intoxicate, but sometimes it cannot find any brain to which to go." In fact, there is just about as much alcohol in a drink of beer as there is in a drink of whisky. The usual drink of whisky is contained in a glass about the height of one's little finger. This drink may be taken straight, followed by water, or diluted, when it becomes a highball. Whisky is about forty per cent alcohol. A drink of wine is about three times as large and contains from ten to thirteen per cent alcohol. A drink of beer is about eight times as large and contains five per cent alcohol. So the quantity of alcohol consumed in one average drink is about the same whether the liquor taken is whisky, wine, or beer.

The teaching of history.—If, in fact, beer and wine are not intoxicating, there was no intoxication known to the world before 800 A. D. We know that intoxication was a major influence in history long before that time. Every reference to drunkenness, every condemnation of it in the Bible refers to beer and wine drunkenness. Noah, the first "drunk" of Bible times, became intoxicated on wine. The drunkenness of Egypt was chiefly due to the consumption of beer. Wine was responsible for the beastly character of Nero's feasts, and Alexander the Great died drunk because of his fondness for barley beer and light wine. It follows, then, that Congress could not pass a law permitting the sale of these intoxicating liquors without violation of the constitutional amendment.

A different day.—Even if the experiment of biblical times supported the argument that it is the abuse of light wines and beer, not their use, which is reprehensible, we must remember that we are dealing with a modern problem. In the time of Jesus in Palestine filth that is now disposed of through modern sewerage systems was tossed from the windows into the street. Shallow wells spread disease, and water was considered positively dangerous, as it is to-day in some countries where similar social conditions exist. It may be that in the Saviour's time it was better to drink wine than to run the risk of typhoid by drinking water contaminated by filth; but to-day in America pure water may be had in abundance.

The experience of Germany and France.—Opponents of prohibition tell us that France and Germany have no liquor problem; that innocent, childlike peasants drink vast quantities of beer and wine, are never drunk, and are free from all the dangers of alcoholism. Germans and Frenchmen are not aware of this ideal state of affairs in Europe. There are in both of these countries vigorous temperance movements directed against the alcoholism traceable to the use of beer and wine.

Alcoholism in France.—In France not only do the people absorb an appalling amount of alcohol in the wine they drink, but the consumption of stronger liquors is greater per capita than it has been in the United States within the present generation. The amount of brandy manufactured by the peasants from their own material is astonishing. Doctor Dupré, *Médécin des Hôpitaux,* has asserted:

Alcoholism, agent in all physical and moral degeneration, is, under the eyes of an indifferent and powerless government, moving on to the destruction of our land. I cannot too much insist on the literal truth of the sorrowful prediction and I affirm that one can inscribe this formula over all the drink shops of France: "Finis Galliæ."

Beer alcoholism in Germany.—In Germany we find that

beer has failed to "solve the problem." Dr. Hugo Hoppe, the famous nerve specialist of Germany, declares:

> The result of extolling beer as the mightiest enemy of whisky and brandy has been that the consumption of distilled liquors has changed very little, while to these liquors has been added beer, the use of which has led to a great and still increasing beer alcoholism.

"KEEP-BEER PROHIBITION"

Our own experience.—Few Americans know that we have tried "keep-beer prohibition" ourselves. In 1858 Iowa, nominally under prohibition, decided to allow the sale of beer and wines. The saloons sold whisky under cover of the beer trade. Massachusetts was under prohibition in 1869. In 1870 the law was amended to allow the sale of ales, porter, beer, and cider. Drunkenness and crime immediately increased. In Boston the number committed to the city prison was nearly twenty-five hundred greater in the year in which the sale of beer was permitted by the State.

The Georgia experiment.—The most recent "keep-beer prohibition" experiment was in Georgia. Georgia intended to pass a real prohibition law but was one of the first to mount the late wave and lacked experience in writing its statutes. In time the law degenerated into a "keep-beer prohibition" measure; and while there was distinct improvement over the old saloon status, the cities of the State were able to flout the law, as it was nearly impossible to keep the beer saloons from selling whisky. When Georgia finally tightened its prohibition law to include beer, the results were notably beneficent. So pleased was the State with the inclusive prohibition law that when the federal government passed its bone-dry act, Georgia was not content to await the date of its operation but overwhelmed its prohibition government with the sentiment for a State bone-dry law to go into effect immediately.

PROBABLE RESULTS OF A BEER-AND-WINE POLICY

Practical aspects of the matter.—America, however, taking all of the circumstances and facts into consideration, faces certain practical aspects of this proposition. If we were to discard prohibition in favor of a beer-and-wine policy, would we be free from the evils of the saloon, which all admit should not be allowed to return? Would we conserve all the economic benefits of prohibition, which all admit to be great? Would we strengthen our political organization and our social structure? It may be right to restore the sale of beer and wine in the United States; but before it is done, the American people ought to realize the following probable results:

A huge liquor bill.—In the section in Chapter VII entitled "What This Waste Would Be To-day" we learned that to destroy prohibition would mean a liquor bill of five billion dollars annually. When the nation closed the saloons, our drink bill was nearly two billion five hundred million dollars. The postwar drink bill in Great Britain, with about forty million people, was found to be approximately double what it was before the outbreak of the war. With increased prices and greater consumption, due to afterwar tendencies, there is no doubt that our liquor bill would be five billion annually, not including the incidental losses to the people caused by the renewed traffic. What would it mean to take five billion dollars out of legitimate American industry at the present time? According to Charles Lennon, of the American Federation of Labor, the working men of the United States contributed seventy per cent to the drink bill in preprohibition days. What would it mean to lower the standard of living of our people, particularly of our working men, to the tune of three billion five hundred million dollars at one time?

The return of the saloon.—We should have the saloon back. The American saloon was a beer saloon, not a whisky saloon. All its institutional evils, including its brothel accompaniment, its gambling hells, and its side entrances for women, introduced by the brewery-owned saloon, would thrive just as well if not a drop of whisky were sold.

The return of alcoholism.—More than ninety per cent of the old-time liquor trade would come back. The belief that beer should not come under the condemnation meted out to whisky is traceable to the common impression that beer drinkers consume much less alcohol than whisky drinkers. But those who believe this overlook the fact that the man who drinks four-per-cent beer usually takes ten times as much as the man who drinks forty-per-cent whisky. The United States Internal Revenue Commissioner, on page 675 of the statistical abstract for 1914, gives the per-capita consumption of distilled spirits and beer for that year, and their respective alcoholic content as follows:

	Gallons used	Gallons of alcohol
Distilled spirits	1.46	0.584
Malt liquors	20.51	0.820

It will be seen from this that the per-capita consumption of alcohol by beer drinkers in 1914 was forty per cent greater than by whisky drinkers.

The return of whisky.—But we should also have whisky back. You cannot open two hundred thousand saloons in this country and keep them from selling whisky. The saloon never obeyed any law passed for its regulation except the law compelling it to pay a tax, and the evasions of that were notorious.

The return of an illicit trade.—We should have the trade back. If you want to know what this was, read the report of the Senate Judiciary Committee on the breweries and anti-American propaganda. All the rottenness and hyphenism of the trade would be once again injected into politics.

A new evil.—We should have a new evil in widespread drinking by women. The American woman was kept out of the American saloon. The American man considered her too good for the debauching influence of beer. Very few respectable women drank at all in America in the old days. But the old standards of conduct for women are passing away under the influence of the new feminism, and we have not yet had time for the establishment of new standards. In this transition time the influence of the saloon and the beer trade, urged by an economic motive and pushed by every method of trade promotion, would be perilous to American womanhood.

Should the Government Sell Liquor?

The case for a government monopoly.—You will remember that we traced the liquor evil to four distinct sources—the psycho-physical, the social, the economic, and the political. Some well-meaning people have thought that if the government were to take over the liquor business itself, at least the economic evil would cease to be a factor, and the government could distribute liquors in such a way as to minimize the social motive of the liquor trade. They tell us of the success of such a system in Sweden, and just at present they are pointing to Quebec as the example to America.

Sweden's experience.—It is true that from 1865 to 1914 Sweden did have a semigovernment-control system. The traffic was taken out of private hands and put into the hands of companies supposed to represent the government and to administer the business in a disinterested way, these companies receiving only a small profit, the remainder of the income going to the state. According to theory this system prevented the pushing of the sale of liquors and the selling of drink to men who had already taken too much. It insured that only "pure" liquor was to be sold, and that places of sale were to be kept clean and orderly. The consumption of brandy and spirits did decrease by 18 per cent between 1865 and 1913; but the sale of wine increased 181 per cent and of beer 240 per cent, and the arrests for drunkenness increased 544 per cent! This shows how encouragingly the sale of wine and beer stops drunkenness. By 1914 the failure of the Gothenburg system was so complete and obvious that the so-called Bratt system was substituted. This further restricted the sale of liquors on the premises and introduced a rationing system for distilled liquors. Every citizen over twenty-one years old could get a pass book permitting him to have a certain amount of distilled liquors each month. The pass-book system itself, however, was an invitation to drink, and the number issued increased from 794,000 in 1916 to more than a million in 1920. The Bratt system was declared a failure by the Swedish Temperance Commission, which studied it for ten years and which eventually declared that prohibition was the only solution of the problem.

South Carolina's experiment.—Not all of us know that we tried a similar system in South Carolina, where it was called the "dispensary." That State voted for prohibition, but the Legislature of 1893 was rebellious and established the dispensary instead. This was intended to take the trade out of private hands, to retain the entire profit for the State, and to reduce the consumption of liquor. It was required that the liquor be sold in sealed packages, that it could not be drunk on the premises, that every customer must make a written application for what he desired to obtain. No liquor could be sold between sunset and sunrise. The system was a terrible failure. In a sense the economic motive was destroyed, but the political motive was intensified. While men could not gather in a dispensary to drink they bought the liquor there and gathered to drink it somewhere else. Blind tigers multiplied, crime increased, and in 1915 the people overwhelmingly passed a prohibition law, which was advocated by Senator Ben Tillman, himself the originator of the dispensary scheme. Saskatchewan in Canada had a similar experience.

The situation in Quebec.—We are hearing more of Quebec to-day than any other place where similar experiments are being tried. In 1919 Quebec carried a referendum for the sale of "light wines and beer." Conditions soon became scandalous, and the government introduced the principle of government ownership and control. There never was more drinking in Montreal and other wet spots of Quebec than there is to-day. Drink has entered the homes to an extent never known in the days of the barroom. Men drink in hotels, cafeterias, restaurants, and clubs. It is not true that there is no drunkenness in Quebec. On the contrary, A. C. Macdonald, who investigated conditions for the *Ladies' Home Journal* and reported his experience in an article entitled "Whirlpools of Beer," says there were more than twelve thousand convictions for drunkenness in two years in Montreal, and that these were of men and women not just ordinarily drunk but "lying drunk in a public street or public place."

He saw hundreds of young girls drinking in cabarets and clubs between midnight and morning and found fully one third of them drunk. The sale of wine and beer under "government control" in Quebec has brought in all of the typical evils of the liquor traffic.

QUESTIONS FOR DISCUSSION

What is the significance of the wet confession that the saloon license system was a failure?

How much did the brewers or the wets do to reform or abolish the saloon before prohibition?

What is the teaching of history as to the intoxicating qualities of wine and beer?

Does the fact that fermentation is natural justify the use of alcoholic beverages?

How does the problem to-day differ from the problem of Christ's day and the problem in this country of a hundred years ago?

What is the experience of France and Germany with wine and beer?

What have been our own experiences with a beer-and-light-wine regime in Iowa, in Georgia, in Massachusetts?

What practical benefits of prohibition would be destroyed by the return of the beer trade in any form whatever?

How do you think the Swedish system would work in this country?

How about the experience of Quebec?

Finally, be strong in the Lord, and in the strength of his might. Put on the whole armor of God, that ye may be able to stand against the wiles of the devil. For our wrestling is not against flesh and blood, but against the principalities, against the powers, against the world-rulers of this darkness, against the spiritual *hosts* of wickedness in the heavenly *places*. Wherefore take up the whole armor of God, that ye may be able to withstand in the evil day, and, having done all, to stand. Stand therefore, having girded your loins with truth, and having put on the breastplate of righteousness, and having shod your feet with the preparation of the gospel of peace; withal taking up the shield of faith, wherewith ye shall be able to quench all the fiery darts of the evil *one*. And take the helmet of salvation, and the sword of the Spirit, which is the word of God: with all prayer and supplication praying at all seasons in the Spirit, and watching thereunto in all perseverance and supplication for all the saints. (Eph. 6. 10-18.)

CHAPTER XII

THE CHRISTIAN AND THE LAW

The liquor traffic can never be legalized without sin. It is vicious in principle, utterly inconsistent with the purpose of enlightened government, and in practice a protection of a traffic which is inherently criminal in its nature.—*General Conference, Methodist Episcopal Church.*

THE status of the fight against the drink evil is to-day an inspiring challenge to lovers of God and humanity. The victory achieved is one of the greatest in significance of all history. The possibilities of the situation point to complete triumph.

THE SITUATION TO-DAY

Prohibition's achievements.—We must include in the tale of accomplishments the abolition of the saloon and the disorganization of the trade. The corner grogshop, as we have known it for generations, is gone. The breweries and distilleries have been curbed. Nearly all the institutions for treatment of confirmed drunkards, such as the Keeley cures, are closed, and their passing is an eloquent comment upon the argument that prohibition has accomplished nothing. Prosperity is with us, and to a very considerable extent it is prohibition prosperity. The social benefits are witnessed by authoritative testimony.

Resistance to the law.—On the other hand, we should be foolish indeed to ignore the fact that there is resistance to the law upon the part of a minority; that the bootleg trade is widespread, conducted by unscrupulous and exceedingly dangerous criminals, supported by "good" citizens whose thoughtless selfishness plagues the country; that wholesale propaganda, having for its purpose the stabilizing of a condition of nullification, with eventual repeal of the law as a result, has affected dry sentiment, even in centers where the evils of the liquor trade had been almost eradicated by local effort.

An unfavorable trend.—Nor should we wince at realization of the undoubted fact that after the immediate phenomenal demonstrations of the value of the prohibition law afforded by the statistics of the first prohibition year, there has been until recently an unfavorable trend, indicating that we have not held our own since the first happy months of 1920. We have a right to be cheered because this reaction has itself begun to react, the statistics indicating that we are once more fighting our way back to better things. Such has been the history of State prohibition in times past. The passage of the prohibition law has always resulted in social and economic benefits of almost startling character. Then, as the enemies of the law and those having a financial profit in its violation began to adapt themselves to unfavorable legal conditions, the evils of drink have reappeared—never to the extent of the period before prohibition but still to a degree that caused chagrin and distress among church people. But prohibitionists, realizing that possession of the law is nine tenths of the battle, have always reconsidered the situation, changed their methods to fit the new conditions, and in time have succeeded in reducing the evil to the minimum.

In control of Congress.—As a nation to-day we occupy a strategic position behind the ramparts of the law, nor is it probable that we will lose our strong hold upon that legal fortress within the near future. Prohibition is in control of the present Congress by a two-thirds majority, and we are not apprehensive that this majority will be even lessened. The constitutional law cannot be changed and will not be; and the wets must capture Congress before they can hope to enact statutory legislation out of harmony with the constitutional provision. In brief, we may claim that we have won the legislative branch of the government, and that permanently.

Executive and judicial failures.—But our government is threefold in character. We have not won complete control of the executive or judicial administration of the law. Mr. Coolidge, while favorable to law enforcement, was never identified with the prohibition movement. Nor was Harding or Wilson. The Secretary of the Treasury is not a convinced prohibitionist. Many men charged with prohibition enforcement are themselves not only opposed to the law but drink the liquors the distribution of which they are under oath to prevent. In the realm of the judiciary wet politicians frequently sit on the bench to try prohibition cases, which are prosecuted by wet district attorneys, handling warrants issued by wet commissioners and executed by wet marshals. We have taken a trench, but position after position lies ahead to be captured.

THE OBLIGATION OF THE CHRISTIAN

On the basis of brotherhood.—The law of the Kingdom is love. God is our Father, and all men are brothers. How does the law of the Kingdom apply to the present situation? The prohibition law assails the menace of alcohol, "against which the human will is as powerless as it is against disease germs." This enslaving drug, beyond controversy, menaces the weak, the poor, the helpless, the unfortunate. The selfish man says, "Why should I be deprived of my drink because some men do not know how to drink or leave it alone?" The Christian says: "I will not indulge if that indulgence results in death and disaster to my fellow man, though I may be able to stop at the moderation point. I will not help to maintain by patronage an institution that wrongs childhood, distresses womanhood, and drags down human life to the level of the brute."

"Personal liberty."—It is not out of place to amplify the discussion of "personal liberty." The selfish man may feel that the prohibition law is an invasion of his personal rights, but how does his personal liberty to drink affect his wife and children, not to speak of the wives and children of his neighbors? How does it affect the right of the community to be free from disorder? How does his selfishness affect your right to conditions which conduce to health and prosperity? The faulty character of the personal-rights claim has been recognized by courts and authority time and again. In the Supreme Court decision in the case of Crowley *versus* Christensen the following may be found:

Even liberty itself, the greatest of all rights, is not unrestricted license to act according to one's own will. It is only freedom from restraint under conditions essential to the same enjoyment of the same right by others. It is, then, liberty regulated by law.

Social restrictions.—Every civilized man is born like the bee—subject to the law of the hive. The license laws were just as much a violation of personal liberty as total prohibition. All the restrictions upon the sale of whisky were arbitrary and artificial, though they were necessary. Says Dr. H. W. Wiley:

The principle of free speech is well established, but free speech which incites to riot and bloodshed is not permitted even in this free country.

If one insists on eating poisoned food and giving it to his family he threatens the existence of the state. If one should choose to walk the streets naked he would offend the rights of other people and thus threaten society.

The principle goes even further. Your body is certainly yours, but if you try to kill it you will go to jail. Sanitary legislation regarding the length of sheets in hotels, public roller towels, public drinking cups, and spitting on sidewalks is merely a recognition of the right of the people to public safety and protection from careless or evil-disposed people, who imagine it to be their personal privilege to spread filth and disease in places frequented by the public.

The Obligation of the Methodist

John Wesley and wine drinking.—As Methodists our obligation is peculiar and insistent. John Wesley was one of the first enemies of the liquor traffic. In regard to wine drinking he said:

You see the wine when it sparkles in the cup and are going to drink it. I say, there is poison in it and therefore beg you to throw it away. If you add, "It is not poison to me, though it may be to others," then I say, Throw it away for thy brother's sake, lest thou embolden him to drink also. Why should thy strength occasion thy weak brother to perish, for whom Christ died?

Wesley's arraignment of liquor sellers.—In 1760 he arraigned liquor sellers in these words:

All who sell liquors in the common way, to any that will buy, are poisoners general. They murder His Majesty's subjects by wholesale; neither does their eye pity or spare. They drive them to hell like sheep. And what is their gain? Is it not the blood of these men? Who, then, would envy their large estates and sumptuous palaces? A curse is in the midst of them. The curse of God is in their gardens, their groves— a fire that burns to the nethermost hell. Blood, blood is there! The foundation, the floors, the walls, the roof, are stained with blood!

As true sons and daughters of Wesley the Methodist Church has ever been foremost in the war to outlaw the trade in drink.

THE OBLIGATION OF CITIZENSHIP

True patriotism in action.—Patriotism demands that we contribute to the strength of the country, if necessary, at the expense of our personal desires. Young China has a motto "That China may be strong," and we would do well to make it ours. Our country can have no strength if we disregard the obligation to uphold democratic decisions, to maintain the practical results of our form of government. In the words of Woodrow Wilson: "I can never accept any man as a champion of liberty who does not reverence the laws of our beloved land. He has adopted the standards of the enemies of his country, whom he affects to despise."

The obligation of the citizen was forcibly stated by President Harding in one of the last of his public utterances:

It is the partial indulgence which challenges the majesty of the law, but the greater crime is the impairment of the moral fibre of the Republic. . . . I do not see how any citizen who cherishes the protection of the law in organized society may feel himself secure when he himself is the example of contempt for law. Ours must be a law-abiding republic, and reverence and obedience must spring from the influential and the leaders among us as well as obedience from the humbler citizen, else the temple will collapse.

Whatever satisfaction there may be in indulgence, whatever objection there is to the so-called invasion of personal liberty, neither counts when the supremacy of law and the stability of our constitutions are menaced.

With all good intention the majority sentiment of the United States has sought by law to remove strong drink as a curse upon the American citizen, but ours is the larger problem now, to remove lawless drinking as a menace to the republic.

America a reservoir of strength.—Despite our wealth of abounding resources there is still poverty and ignorance to be banished. We need all of our wealth of material and manhood if our civilization is even to approximate the ideal. America should and must be a reservoir of strength and of moral power for the benefit of the entire world, and this it cannot be until we are free of drink's handicap.

THE OBLIGATION OF PROSPERITY

A great deal of drinking is by men who are prosperous but who are without the education and heritage that would give them standards to uphold. Most of them drink because they have heard or read that it is "smart" to do so. The man whom rude energy and peculiar gifts have made a millionaire, who fills his cellar with wines and liquor, who says that prohibition is a good thing for the laboring man but means nothing to him, should remember that his real property, his stocks and bonds, even the safety of his wife and children, depend upon the prestige of the law. Every dollar the man has made he made under the law's protection. For him to profit by law's ascendency and then strike at the very foundations of law is not only selfishness supreme but reckless folly.

The harm done by so-called "respectable citizens" who violate the law is thus bluntly stated by Governor Gifford Pinchot:

It is not the solemn ass who gets up in assemblage and solemnly announces that "prohibition cannot be enforced." It is not the flappers and "sheiks," who rather take to the idea that it is clever and devilish to break the law. I don't mean those, either, of permanently immature minds who seem to be congenitally incapable of thinking there is anything more sacred than a cocktail before dinner. These folks do some harm, but not much.

The real harm is done by able, influential people of the community who set themselves on the side of the bootlegger and against the law. All that is necessary to straighten them out is to have them come to a realizing sense of what they are doing.

The Obligation of Youth

Youth facing the same problem.—What are the young people going to do in the crisis of to-day? Many of them have never seen a saloon and are utterly unacquainted with the evils of the license days. The educational propaganda that prompted the preceding generation to arise in might against the saloon has to a considerable extent lapsed, since the law was thought to register a final solution of the problem. Yet the youth of to-day must pass upon the problem as our fathers passed upon it in their day. The responsibility cannot be evaded.

An unsupported claim.—It is frequently claimed that the young people of to-day, so far from realizing any such responsibility, are drinking more than ever before. Certainly they are drinking too much; but try to remember what the conditions were before prohibition. In that day a saloon was open on nearly every corner, and nearly every high-school boy in our cities patronized the saloons more or less. Invitations to drink were frequent, and when the boy learned to drink he was usually introduced to worse habits. To-day youth may drink, but the only stuff available is vile and it costs ten prices. It is not reasonable to believe that young people under such conditions consume one tenth as much liquor as they did when the product and the trade were as attractive as they could well be. A questionnaire sent to the high-school principals of Massachusetts by the Scientific Temperance Federation brought the almost unanimous reply from these experienced leaders of youth that there is much less drinking among young people than in former years. Professor Gilbert J. Raynor, principal of the Alexander Hamilton High School, Brooklyn, making a statement upon this subject, says that in four years he has not observed a single case of violation of the prohibition law among the nearly four thousand pupils in his school. About a year ago one of the New York City newspapers took a straw vote in a senior class of that high school on prohibition. The vote stood 229 against modification of the prohibition law to 5 for it. We must not be misled by superficial indications.

THE OBLIGATION TO OURSELVES

The temple of his body.—You remember that it is said of Christ, "But he spake of the temple of his body." In this day, when sport occupies such a large place in American life, we all realize the necessity of caring for our bodies if we are to be efficient and happy. This consideration in the early days of temperance reform was most often advanced as an argument in favor of abstinence. Certainly the abstainer has all the better of it. He lives longer, his health is better, he has more of the flowing vitality which makes for the joy of life. It is not a sin to eat too much salad and be ill; it is a mistake. But to make a practice of making oneself ill with foods that are clearly injurious is certainly something more than a mistake, and to eat such foods for a drug effect, regardless of the fact of their admitted injurious character, certainly ignores the teaching of Christ that our bodies are the temples of the Holy Spirit. There is a Christian obligation to personal health and cleanliness in so far as we can attain to these things by our efforts.

It pays to do right.—There is another personal consideration. The Bible teaches, and experience proves, that it pays to do right. Shallow magazine writers, whose success in a special field indicates nothing as to general experience, frequently create the impression that drinking is necessary to social and business success. On the contrary, it is almost fatal to business success; and its social value is greatly overestimated if it exists at all. The business world is suspicious of the man who takes liquor under any circumstances; and in society, so called, almost everyone is ready to respect the man or woman with the independence and confidence in his own standards indicated by a refusal to drink liquors. Such refusal probably will not even be noticed at all; and when it is noticed, it is usually with approval.

QUESTIONS FOR DISCUSSION

Reviewing the facts of former lessons, what do you think are some of the bright spots in the situation to-day? What are some of the reasons for concern? Do these reasons put a question mark after the value of prohibition?

What may we expect in regard to the development of prohibition enforcement in view of the experience of prohibition States? What is our greatest element of strength?

Is the prohibition law in harmony with the Christian law of love? What is the heritage of opinion of the Methodists in regard to this matter? What is the obligation of prosperity?

To what extent are young people drinking to-day? Do you think they are drinking more or less than before prohibition? Do you believe drinking is a social liability or an asset?

Our Father who art in heaven, Hallowed be thy name. Thy kingdom come. Thy will be done, as in heaven, so on earth. Give us this day our daily bread. And forgive us our debts, as we also have forgiven our debtors. And bring us not into temptation, but deliver us from the evil *one*. (Matt. 6. 9b-13.)

CHAPTER XIII

HOW TO HELP

The eyes of the world are upon the United States. What Kansas and North Dakota did for us, America will do for the nations—that is, show that a great people can grow and prosper, educate their children, run their government, pay their debts, and build mighty institutions without the help of a single tainted dollar of liquor revenue.—*Clarence True Wilson.*

THE first and most important assistance the Christian citizen can give to the war on drink is to obey the law. The four square inches in front of every man's mouth can be made absolute prohibition territory if he allows his conscience to rule his life. Law enforcement is good. Law observance is infinitely better. Law enforcement should be for criminals and other foes of society. Law observance should be the tribute that the Christian pays to righteous government.

HAVE FAITH IN THE LAW

An impregnable theory.—There never has been a fact to shake the validity of the prohibition policy. Prohibition cannot be criticized with justice. The theory is impregnable. Prohibition administration may and should be criticized.

A social measure.—If you have a prejudice against illegitimate coercion, retain it. It does not run counter to the prohibition theory. Prohibition does not prevent the individual from injuring himself; it prevents him from injuring others. He does not have to become drunk to inflict injury upon society. His indulgence in drink itself inevitably injures the common welfare. Opponents tell us that the drink trade *might* be conducted without harm to society. Sufficient answer is that in the thousands of years of experience with it, it *has not* been so conducted. Prohibition as a foundation for proper governmental procedure against the evil should be accepted as permanently established.

Understand the Work to Be Done

Thoughtless selfishness.—If we are to defend the prohibition policy with success we must take human nature into consideration. What motive, for instance, animates the youth who places a flask of whisky in his hip pocket and proceeds to his school dance? Why does the "new-rich" man indulge freely and conspicuously? These questions were put to a Sunday-school class recently and evoked various answers: "Just pure meanness." "They want to show off." "They don't know what they are doing." Each answer is correct. It is "meanness" in the sense that it is thoughtless selfishness. No one who is not already an alcoholic ever takes bootleg liquor because he likes it. The show-off instinct, manifested by youth and parvenu alike, is an effort to overcome an inferiority complex by showing a contempt for restraint, manifesting an independence of the law. The meanness is selfishness. The thoughtlessness and ignorance are the things to be taken into consideration.

Is dissipation manly?—There is also among young people a strange inclination to think that dissipation is manly. This instinct is rooted in the fact that the child is prevented by authority from indulging in harmful things. When, therefore, he has reached an age when he can indulge without fear of authority he wishes to indicate the fact to the world as evidence of his approaching manhood. The same old inferiority complex again! The truth is that manhood is evidenced by self-control, not by resistance to outside control. The manliest young men do not drink. Many of them do not even smoke. "I have four all-American stars helping me at Michigan University," says "Hurry-up" Yost, one of the greatest football coaches the college world has known. "Among those four assistants there isn't one who has ever taken a drink, ever smoked, ever used profanity, or ever told a dirty story. Are they effeminate? Well, the four of them can take thirty of the other type and break them into a number of pieces without straining a muscle."

olving a personal problem.—Let the young man who
"shows off" with a flask of liquor realize the truth of these
things, and his personal problem will be solved. The
problem of his maladjustment to the law will be solved
with equal ease if he is made to realize the logic of his
position. Convince him that he is not showing his independence of a few fanatics but is showing his independence
of his country—the country that has nurtured and now
protects him, the country he has been taught to love, and
for which he would gladly die. Let him grasp the fact
that by drinking he is helping to augment the swollen
profits of the bootlegger who races through the streets in
contemptuous disregard of human life and is in the
vilest of rebellions against the authority of the United
States. Let him know that by supporting this rebellion
he is helping to give color to the belief cherished by all
lawless minorities that they can destroy authority by
criminal activities against it. The appeal should be made
to conscience, and the result will be gratifying in the
majority of cases.

HELP EDUCATE

The lethargy of Christian people.—Christian people
have been slow to assume their duties in creating and
maintaining a favorable body of comment on the prohibition law. We hear utterly uninformed people speak
against it on every hand, but our mouths remain tightly
shut. Why? Is there any logical reason why we should
not advance our opinion in support of the law when the
opponents are not embarrassed in attacking the law? Anyone who has studied the question for thirteen weeks knows
infinitely more about it than the street-corner wet propa-
gandist who has not studied the problem at all—indeed,
has perhaps never studied any problem. The President of
the United States recently called attention to the duty
of the churches and Christian people generally to educate
and never to cease educating until the law rests upon
nearly universal support.

Antiprohibition propaganda.—The duty of education
was easier before the prohibition law than it is now because the evident and obtrusive facts to be seen on every

hand themselves broke down the counter propaganda of
the wets. Now the wets have a similar advantage. All
the evils of the liquor trade they call the "evils of prohibition," and the people, having forgotten the days of the
saloon, know simply that they want a change from present
conditions. The strategy and duty of the hour, then, is
not only to educate ourselves but to take effective counter-
action against the "education" of the wets. Wet propaganda when it stands on its own feet is ineffective; but
it comes to us from the daily press as misrepresentation,
from the stage as suggestion and ridicule, as well as from
literature, art, and song. The Sunday paper that puts
antiprohibition argument into the mouths of its crudely
comic characters, the cartoon that sneers at the prohibition
law, the jokes based on misinformation, all constitute wet
propaganda of the most formidable character. It will be
claimed that we are without a sense of humor if we take
this position, but nevertheless we are right. How do the
manufacturers of Campbell's Soup advertise their wares?
They pay thousands of dollars for a page in a great magazine upon which to print a verse of doggerel. Do you
think that these business men who pay vast sums of money
to get these senseless verses before the people would do
so if they were without effect? The truth is that the most
effective propaganda works by casual touches. The constant dripping of water wears away stone, and the constant drip-drip of this wet propaganda wears away prohibition conviction. We should protest earnestly when our
favorite newspaper sends into our home sneers and ridicule of the prohibition law, when we pay for entertainment and must listen to antiprohibition jokes, when we
find in a novel a disguised argument in favor of drink.

The Christian Citizen in Action

Demand dry appointments.—Prohibitionists have a
right to control the entire government in behalf of a constitutional policy. No man has a right to expect to be
appointed a United States commissioner, a United States
marshal, a United States judge or district attorney, unless he is a prohibitionist. We should know whom our
dry senator recommends for these positions, and especially

for the police work of the Prohibition Unit. And we should demand that he support the law by recommending only men who are earnestly desirous that it be upheld. The government should and must be a unit in all of its branches against the evil of drink.

Demand State enforcement.—Has your State a prohibition law? Do the local police enforce that law? If your State was dry before prohibition, is it making as great an effort for prohibition enforcement as it did before the amendment or has it lain down on the job and left it all to the federal government? If some "bad actor" in your community is running a blind pig on the corner, should the federal government at Washington be notified to send officers to take care of it? To do such work effectively the federal government would need as many police as are now employed by the States and cities. Your local bootlegger or moonshiner should be taken care of by your local police and courts as a part of their regular duties. This is better from every angle. The closer government is to the people from whom it proceeds, the more effective is its machinery. Demand that the federal government attend to the federal duties of liquor suppression, but demand with ten times as much vigor that your local government do its duty. If your State has no prohibition law, then a fight for such legislation should be made. If the State is hopelessly in the hands of our enemies, then the federal government may logically be called upon to do its best to relieve the loyal American people of that State.

Cooperate with the government.—It is not our duty to enforce the law. Officials are paid to do so and should be compelled to earn their money. But we should cooperate with the government, serving on juries when called, giving accurate information to officers (without, of course, assisting in prosecution), encouraging faithful officials and prodding those who are negligent, occasionally attending court to see just what is going on. We must not believe that prohibition officers as a class are grafters. This is not true. Indeed, few officials are.

Suggestions from the Prohibition Unit.—The Prohibition Unit has made the following suggestions for aiding

law enforcement: (1) Individually: Give your cooperation and assistance to all enforcement officers. Commend
them when faithful. Publicly and privately register your
sentiment in favor of vigorous enforcement of the law.
Serve on juries when called. Express your opinion to the
editor of your paper, commend papers that support the
law, protest when they oppose it. Acquaint yourself with
the facts in order to refute the misrepresentations of wet
propagandists. Keep your daily conduct in strict obedience to the law, thus creating an example to others. (2)
Collectively: As an organization study the national, State,
and city enforcement laws and the names and duties of
the officials who are charged with its enforcement.

Cooperate with enforcement officials.—Confer with the
prosecuting attorney, executive officer, or county judge as
to the best methods of cooperation. Report evidence of law
violations to the local officials whose duty it is to enforce
the law. Keep a complete roster of all law-enforcement officials in your city and county. Send them helpful information, encouraging news items on law enforcement, and
appreciative letters showing your interest in their efforts.
Keep in weekly touch with the local law-enforcement
office to see what is needed. Obtain lists of convictions
and tabulate arrests for drunkenness and crimes from
court dockets and police departments each month or
quarter and report to State enforcement headquarters.
Follow up cases where sentence is suspended during good
behavior and report violations of court order. Notify
prosecuting officers when parties are arrested for second
offense, as, if the fact is proved, a more severe penalty is
provided for such cases. Send evidence to State enforcement headquarters of law violations by permit holders. Information concerning law violations should be given to
owners of buildings when on their premises.

Attend court.—Be present at the first session of the
federal or local court of your district, that you may learn
the attitude of the judge on the question of enforcing the
law. Arrange for representatives of your organization to
attend court trials of important cases.

Protest.—Protest in a dignified manner to the mayor,
prosecutor, judge, or other officer who fails in doing his

duty and makes law enforcement a farce. When public officers fail in doing their duty, a committee can often voice a dignified protest that will bring good results. One should give him every chance to do his full duty, however, before a protest is filed. When public officials ignore their oath of office and fail to enforce the law even though they have the evidence, publish this news in the newspapers and make it widely known to the taxpaying citizens. Protest to theater managers the showing of pictures or scenes that treat the eighteenth amendment lightly. Take the initiative, if it becomes necessary, in calling a mass meeting of citizens to outline a campaign that will result in law observance and law enforcement.

Educate public sentiment.—Ask ministers to preach on law observance. Lose no opportunity for short talks at clubs, Bible classes, Americanization schools, etc. Train the children in the home, the school, and the Sunday school to recognize obedience to authority. Create public sentiment for law by talking it. Whenever the eighteenth amendment is condemned in your presence, speak your convictions courageously but never in anger. Ask your editor for an occasional editorial on law observance. Remember the ringing words of Nehemiah: "Be not ye afraid of them: remember the Lord, who is great and terrible, and fight for your brethren, your sons, and your daughters, your wives, and your houses." (Neh. 4. 14.)

QUESTIONS FOR DISCUSSION

Discuss law enforcement as opposed to law observance.

Do you believe that prohibition is an unwarranted coercion of the individual?

In addition to the reasons given in the book what do you think are some of the reasons why men without a liquor appetite drink?

Do the leaders in your school or in your business drink?

What are some of the practical implications of drink under the present circumstances?

Why do you think Christian people are slow to speak out in defense of their convictions, while their opponents are very free in their expressions?

Can you name some instances of "sneak" propaganda

embodied in humor, song, slang, or fiction? Do you think such propaganda is effective? What is the best way to counteract it?

Is the prohibition administrator of your district wet or dry? How about the federal judge, the district attorney, the United States marshal, the United States commissioners?

What are some of the functions of the federal government in prohibition enforcement? Contrast them with State duties.

Give some methods of cooperation with officials in prohibition enforcement.

BIBLIOGRAPHY

The Case for Prohibition, by Clarence True Wilson and Deets Pickett (Funk & Wagnalls).

Cyclopedia of Temperance, Prohibition, and Public Morals, by Deets Pickett, Clarence True Wilson, and Ernest Dailey Smith (The Methodist Book Concern).

The Allied Reforms, by Deets Pickett and Charles C. Rarick (Board of Temperance, Prohibition, and Public Morals of the Methodist Episcopal Church).

The Wooden Horse, by Deets Pickett (The Abingdon Press).

The Logic of Prohibition, by Matt S. Hughes (Board of Temperance, Prohibition, and Public Morals of the Methodist Episcopal Church).

Dry or Die, by Clarence True Wilson (Board of Temperance, Prohibition, and Public Morals of the Methodist Episcopal Church).

The Divine Right of Democracy, by Clarence True Wilson (The Abingdon Press).

Temperance Sermons, compiled by Clarence True Wilson (The Methodist Book Concern).

Lincoln and Liquor, by Duncan C. Milner (Neale Publishing Company).

Anti-Saloon League Year Book (each year).

How to Live, by Irving Fisher and Eugene L. Fisk (Funk & Wagnalls).

The Action of Alcohol on Man, by Ernest H. Starling (Longmans, Green & Co.).

Laws of Life and Health, by Alexander Bryce (Lippincott).

Prohibition Inside Out, by Roy A. Haynes (Doubleday, Page & Co.).

Alcohol and the Human Body, by Sir Victor Horsley and Mary G. Sturge (Macmillan Company).

Federal Government and the Liquor Traffic, by William E. Johnson (American Issue Publishing Company).

Alcohol and Human Efficiency, by Walter R. Miles (Carnegie Institute of Washington).

Prohibition in America, by Arthur Newsholme (P. S. King & Son).

Social Welfare and the Liquor Problem, by Harry S. Warner (Intercollegiate Prohibition Association, Washington, D. C.).

Prohibition Going or Coming? by Elton R. Shaw (Shaw Publishing Company, Berwyn, Illinois).

The Drink Problem in Its Medio-Sociological Aspects, by Theophilus N. Kelynack (E. P. Dutton & Co.).

The Effect of Alcohol Upon Longevity, by Oscar H. Rogers (New York Life Insurance Company).

National Prohibition Enforcement Manual (Anti-Saloon League).

What Became of the Distilleries, Breweries, and Saloons in the United States? (World League Against Alcoholism, Westerville, Ohio).

The Legalized Outlaw, by Artman (Board of Temperance, Prohibition, and Public Morals of the Methodist Episcopal Church).

Hold Fast, America, by Gifford Gordon (World League Against Alcoholism).

Alcohol in Experience and Experiment, by Cora F. Stoddard (American Issue Publishing Company).

How Prohibition Works in American Cities, by Deets Pickett (Board of Temperance, Prohibition, and Public Morals of the Methodist Episcopal Church).